Our Words, Our Ways:

Teaching First Nations, Métis and Inuit Learners

Alberta Education Cataloguing in Publication Data

Alberta. Alberta Education. Aboriginal Services Branch and Learning and Teaching Resources Branch.
Our words, our ways : teaching First Nations, Métis and Inuit learners.

ISBN 0-7785-4313-7

1. Indians of North America – Education – Alberta. 2. Métis – Education – Alberta.
3. Inuit – Education – Alberta. 4. Education and state – Alberta.
I. Title. II. Alberta. Alberta Education. Learning and Teaching Resources Branch.

E96.65.A3.A333 2005   371.9

For further information, contact:

Aboriginal Services Branch
9th Floor, 44 Capital Boulevard
10044 – 108 Street NW
Edmonton, Alberta T5J 5E6
Telephone: 780–415–9300 in Edmonton or
toll-free in Alberta by dialing 310–0000
Fax: 780–415–9306

Learning and Teaching Resources Branch
8th Floor, 44 Capital Boulevard
10044 – 108 Street NW
Edmonton, Alberta T5J 5E6
Telephone: 780–427–2984 in Edmonton or
toll-free in Alberta by dialing 310–0000
Fax: 780–422–0576

The primary intended audience for this document is:

Teachers	✓
Administrators	✓
School Staff	✓
Counsellors	✓
Liaison Workers	✓
Students	
Parents	
General Public	

 A PDF version of this resource is available on the Alberta Education Web site at www.education.gov.ab.ca/k_12/curriculum/other.asp

Print copies of this resource can be purchased from the Learning Resources Centre. Order online at www.lrc.education.gov.ab.ca/ or telephone 780–427–2767.

Table of Contents

Acknowledgements

We would like to acknowledge the wisdom and foresight of our ancestors who signed Treaties 4, 6, 7, 8 and 10 so future generations would have an education, and participate in and contribute to Canadian society as First Nations, Métis and Inuit people. We dedicate this resource to them.

– Tracey Poitras-Collins, Project Manager of *Our Words, Our Ways*
Aboriginal Services Branch, Alberta Education

Aye-aye, ki na nâ sko mi tin nâwaw, nii tsii ksik ksii ma tsi tsiip, mahsi, marci, merci, thank you to the community Elders, teachers, parents, guardians, and other individuals and groups who contributed to the development of this resource, including the following.

Gatherers and sharers of information from Edmonton Catholic Schools' Aboriginal Learning Centre
Louise Breland, Carola Cunningham, Ken Ealey, Toni Kalita, Shirley Mykituk, Bev Ross, Bob Steele

Principal writer
Marnie Robb

Contributing writer
Crystal M. John

Index
Judy Dunlop Information Services

Cover design concept
Warren Starr-Yellowknee (www.warrenstarryellowknee.netfirms.com)

Alberta Education
Aboriginal Services Branch
Evelyn Good Striker	Acting Director
Patsy Steinhauer	Education Manager

Learning and Teaching Resources Branch
Raja Panwar	Director
Greg Bishop	Assistant Director
Catherine Walker	Resource Manager
Doris Gladue	Resource Manager
Sandra Mukai	Copyright
Dianne Moyer	Document Production

Special thanks to: Special Programs Branch, Rick Hayes, Lorraine Stewart and Rebecca Pound

Welcome

This resource will help classroom teachers and staff better serve the needs of their Aboriginal students. The process of development was one of consultation, information gathering, drafting, more consultation and re-drafting. The contributors to this resource include Aboriginal Elders, teachers and psychologists as well as other members of Alberta's Aboriginal communities.

Culturally-relevant approaches effectively serve the learning needs of Aboriginal students. The term Aboriginal refers to the descendants of the original inhabitants of North America. The Canadian Constitution recognizes three groups of Aboriginal peoples: First Nations, Métis and Inuit. Traditional and contemporary Aboriginal cultures offer a number of frameworks for understanding, guiding, learning from and teaching students.

The relationship between student and teacher is the heart of Aboriginal education. The teacher's relationship with each student is based on observing and learning about the individual child and his or her unique learning needs in order to help the child grow holistically—spiritually, physically, mentally and emotionally. Education is very important to Aboriginal people—it is a key to the future for Aboriginal children and their families.

This resource offers information about Aboriginal cultures and perspectives, practical ideas, and sample strategies that will help teachers meet the needs and recognize the gifts of Aboriginal students. Many of the sample strategies are good for all students and are relevant for a range of educational settings and contexts.

Guiding Principles

- Teacher understanding of and respect for the diversities of Aboriginal cultures, languages, histories and worldviews is integral to the success of Aboriginal students.

- Creating a classroom atmosphere that reflects and respects Aboriginal perspectives will benefit all the students in the classroom.

- Teacher/student relationship is the foundation of that student's success in the classroom.

- Teacher recognition and continued assessment of the learning strengths and needs of each Aboriginal student is vital to that student's progress.

- Positive, collaborative relationships with the families and communities of Aboriginal students will support student success.

Defining family

Extended families and guardian relationships are a well-established part of Aboriginal community life. The term "parent" in this resource refers to the person taking the role of involved adult in a student's life. This person could be a grandparent, aunt, uncle, older sibling, cousin or other family member. Adoption is also common in Aboriginal communities—often in a social rather than legal sense—where an individual is "adopted" or "taken in" by a family, clan or community.

How this Resource is Organized

The resource is organized into seven chapters. Each chapter contains information, sample strategies, shared wisdom from Aboriginal scholars and Elders, and related stories shared by Aboriginal teachers and liaisons.

Worldviews and Aboriginal Cultures: Where hearts are rooted

Worldviews permeate all aspects of effective education of Aboriginal students. Worldviews are like stones thrown into the water from which other circles grow. Learning about the traditional and contemporary experiences unique to each Aboriginal student helps to develop effective approaches for supporting that student in the classroom. An understanding of Aboriginal history can help teachers contribute to the process of rebuilding healthy Aboriginal communities in which education is built on an acceptance and respect for Aboriginal languages, cultures and worldviews.

Aboriginal Students: Who are they? How do they learn?

All Aboriginal students are unique individuals with their own set of gifts and needs, as well as members of a family and a cultural community. A teacher's best source of information about a student's gifts and needs grows out of a collaborative relationship with the student. By observing, experiencing and reflecting in partnership with the student, a teacher can learn how to most effectively support the student's success in the classroom.

The Classroom: A community of learners

Aboriginal student learning is enhanced by a safe, comfortable classroom environment—a community of learners. Aboriginal students do their best work when they experience:

- a sense of belonging as respected and valued students
- the spirit of mastery that comes through encouragement of their gifts and competencies
- independence developed by opportunities to develop inner control and responsibility
- the spirit of generosity that reflects core values of sharing and community responsibility (Brendtro, Brokenleg and Van Bockern 1990).

School, Family and Community: Sharing the responsibility

Parents play a vital part in an Aboriginal student's education, providing support, insight and direction. Welcoming the family, Elders, traditional teachers and others to the school and classroom strengthens Aboriginal students' experiences of cultural continuity as the core of the learning process.

Learning Strategies for Aboriginal Students: Opportunities to make learning meaningful

Learning strategies, tailored to reflect cultural continuity, support Aboriginal students' success in the classroom.

Assessment: Authentic reflections of important learnings

Culturally-aware classroom assessment and grading practices provide Aboriginal students with appropriate opportunities to demonstrate their learning.

Teaching Aboriginal Students with Learning Disabilities: Recognizing gifts and strengths

Traditional Aboriginal worldviews recognize that each person brings a unique set of gifts to the community. Rather than regarding a student's learning challenges as disabilities, traditional approaches encourage the student and those who guide him or her to value both learning strengths and challenges.

Chapter 1

Worldviews and Aboriginal Cultures:
Where hearts are rooted

This chapter will help teachers to:
- gain an increased appreciation of the histories and cultural diversity of Aboriginal students
- gain a better understanding of the unique worldviews of Aboriginal students
- recognize the importance of reflecting the worldviews, strengths and gifts of Aboriginal cultures in the classroom through a consistent emphasis on cultural continuity
- recognize patterns of cultural differences
- begin to take steps to learn and teach about Aboriginal peoples.

Aboriginal students, regardless of whether they are gifted, bright, average or struggling, come to the classroom with histories and worldviews that are unique. Because these are such an integral part of who they are, it may be difficult for parents and students to articulate exactly what their histories and worldviews are, and exactly how these factors affect what they think and do. Some students in urban centres may have limited contact and understanding of their Aboriginal culture.

Even students who are assimilated into the mainstream culture, or who do not strongly identify with their Aboriginal ancestry, may face racism or be confronted with stereotypes. In order to avoid racism and stereotyping, some Aboriginal children make a concerted effort to hide their Aboriginal identity, claiming to be French, Italian—anything but Aboriginal.

While Aboriginal students benefit from best teaching practices, teachers support their students' learning needs most effectively when they incorporate into their teaching practice an understanding of the two key concepts in this chapter: Aboriginal histories and Aboriginal worldviews.

Understanding the history and the cultures of the Aboriginal peoples in the local community creates a better understanding of Aboriginal students. Becoming more familiar with Aboriginal worldviews helps teachers build cultural continuity into both the content and instructional approaches of all subject areas. Part of effectively learning about other cultures is developing a deeper understanding of your own culture. Becoming more aware of how cultural beliefs and practices affect teaching practices will help individual teachers make better and more culturally responsive choices throughout the teaching day.

Strategies for Understanding History

The first—and most important—step towards understanding Aboriginal history is to recognize that Aboriginal people are strong people. In spite of the severity of the many issues that individuals, families and communities face, Aboriginal people are demonstrating their resiliency.

The shared history between Aboriginal peoples and European settlers is one of cultural disruption. Generations of Aboriginal peoples experienced profound, unsought and irreversible changes in their cultural and family life as a result. Many Aboriginal people are working to change the cycles of abuse, the social and economic disruption, the loss of languages and the assimilation of their cultures.

Education is a key to this change. Aboriginal people are building bridges and working to create educational communities where their children are respected and their cultures are reflected. They are rebuilding their Aboriginal cultures and hope to right the relations of the past.

Key Historical Events for Aboriginal People of Alberta

There are a number of key events in the last two hundred years that affect Aboriginal people today.

The *Indian Act* [1]

In 1876, the government of Canada consolidated the *Gradual Civilization Act* and the *Indian Enfranchisement Act* into a single, comprehensive piece of legislation. The *Indian Act*, though amended over the years in important ways, remains a central fact of life for First Nations people in Canada.

---

1. Reproduced with permission from Kainai Board of Education et al., *Peoples and Cultural Change: Aboriginal Studies 20* (Edmonton, AB: Duval House Publishing Inc., 2005), pp. 54–55.

The *Act* reinforced the powers of Canada's government over First Nations and extended those powers in significant ways. It regulated virtually every aspect of the lives of First Nations people in an effort to promote assimilation.

The *Indian Act* continued to disrupt traditional forms of government. It added new regulations about who qualified as members of a band, which determined who could vote in band elections. The *Indian Act* had a negative impact on the roles of women and Elders in traditional First Nations. Many traditional government practices held women and men as equal participants, and Elders as respected advisors and leaders. After the *Indian Act*, women and Elders were effectively removed from all official processes of government.

The government policy of assimilation led to the restriction of many activities that First Nations people practised in order to transmit their cultures. The *Indian Act's* most significant legacy was to rule and restrict the lives of First Nations people, even though its stated intent was to protect the rights and privileges of the first peoples of Canada.

Residential schools

Under the *Indian Act*, education of First Nations and Inuit peoples became a federal responsibility that was met through the implementation of residential schools. Residential schools were established to assimilate First Nations and Inuit children into the dominant English-speaking, Christian culture. Many of the values and morals of this culture were in conflict with traditional Aboriginal values and customs.

Residential schools were put in place in the 1860s. In 1920, Canada amended the *Indian Act*, making it mandatory for First Nations and Inuit parents to send their children to Indian residential schools. The last residential school in Alberta closed in 1988. The last federally-operated residential school in Canada closed in Saskatchewan in 1996.

Five to six generations of First Nations and Inuit peoples were subjected to the residential school system. Children as young as four were removed from their families and taken to spend the majority of the year in institutions, often far away from their homes. Children were forbidden to speak their language and unable to follow their traditional customs. As a result, they often became ashamed of their language, culture and family. Some parents were forbidden to visit their children and did not see them for several years at a time.

Limited funds meant overcrowding and unhealthy living conditions, and children were exposed to diseases such as tuberculosis. Deputy Superintendent Duncan Campbell Scott estimated that overall "fifty percent of the children who passed through these schools did not live to benefit from the education which they had received therein" (1913, p. 615).

Despite the legislation and the pressures, many First Nations and Inuit people resisted the government's efforts to assimilate their children. Some spoke out directly against the system. Many others simply refused to send their children to school, no matter what the consequences. Attendance remained low, in both residential and day schools. Only 3 percent of First Nations children remained in school beyond Grade 6.[2]

Liz Poitras, a Cree Elder, Sawridge First Nation, relates the following story about how some Aboriginal parents managed to keep their family together during this time. "In 1950 the Indian agent and priest came to my home to take me and my brothers and sisters to residential school. My father stood at the end of our driveway with his rifle and told them that if they came any closer he would shoot them. Needless to say, my brothers, sisters and I did not go to residential school and I am very thankful to my late dad, Albert Potskin, former Sawridge Band Councillor, for doing what he did." Education was important to Liz's family and she went on to get a graduate degree.

Although the federal government did not offer education specifically to Métis people, some Métis families, especially religious families, chose to send their children to residential schools.

While some Aboriginal people report that residential school was a positive experience, many felt a loss of cultural identity, the loss of opportunity to develop parenting skills and the impacts of trauma—all of which affected how they raised their children. The residential school experience has had an extensive impact on many communities.

Even the best-run residential schools and the most dedicated staff inflicted untold damage because of the flawed system. Entire generations of First Nations and Inuit people were essentially deprived of a normal family life. Parents lost the chance to raise their own children, and children lost the love and security of their homes, families and communities. Not only was traditional education of First Nations and Inuit children interfered with, the traditional family structure was broken.[3]

---

2. Reproduced with permission from Kainai Board of Education et al., *Peoples and Cultural Change: Aboriginal Studies 20* (Edmonton, AB: Duval House Publishing Inc., 2005), p. 182.

3. Ibid., pp. 182–183.

The hurt was cultural as well as personal. At residential schools, First Nations and Inuit children were taught that their cultures—their spiritual beliefs, their languages, even the clothes they wore—were inferior and wrong.[3]

A minority of residential school staff deliberately used their positions to abuse students emotionally, physically and sometimes even sexually. Because of their positions of power and the relative powerlessness of their victims, these abusers never expected to have to someday account for their crimes. The sexual abuse that took place in some schools damaged the self-identity of these children, which led to increased violence and suicide in First Nations and Inuit communities.[3]

Many residential school students received an inferior education. Because they spent only half of each day in the classroom, they did not have the same opportunities as other children. In the eyes of the system, First Nations and Inuit people were fit only for menial work. It was considered a waste to prepare them for anything more. Many children left the schools at age eighteen with the equivalent of only a Grade 5 education.[3]

stories

Shared

"The survivors of the Indian residential school system have, in many cases, continued to have their lives shaped by the experiences in these schools. Persons who attended these schools continue to struggle with their identity after years of being taught to hate themselves and their culture. The residential school led to a disruption in the transference of parenting skills from one generation to the next. Without these skills, many survivors had difficulty in raising their own children. In residential schools, they learned that adults often exert power and control through abuse. The lessons learned in childhood are often repeated in adulthood with the result that many survivors of the residential school system often inflict abuse on their own children. These children in turn use the same tools on their children."

Royal Commission on Aboriginal Peoples 1996b, p. 379

Restrictive amendments to the *Indian Act*
In 1884, an amendment to the *Indian Act* instituted prison sentences for anyone participating in potlatch, tawanawa dance and other traditional ceremonies (Royal Commission on Aboriginal Peoples 1996a).

In 1895, further amendments prohibiting traditional dances and customs followed. Practices associated with traditional dances, including the Blackfoot Sundance, and the Cree and Saulteaux thirst dance, were banned.

Following the *Indian Act*, the pass system was introduced. First Nations on the prairies were permitted to leave their reserves only if they had a written pass from a local Indian agent.

In 1924, amendments to the *Indian Act* made it illegal to gather to discuss political and economic issues, including land claims. It was also illegal to raise funds for land claims.

Reserves[4]

One of the key provisions included in every numbered treaty was the creation of reserves. This provision alone had profound consequences for First Nations people. For example, the reserves secured land for First Nations, but could also be used as a way of confining First Nations people. Being confined to a reserve interfered with the traditional economic activities such as hunting and trapping, where it was not possible to remain settled in one small area of land.

Today many First Nations people in Alberta live on these reserves that were negotiated years ago.

Adapting to life on reserves was a major challenge for the First Nations people of the Plains. The idea of staying in one place to farm was contrary to traditional ways of life that involved moving seasonally to take advantage of resources in a wide region. People of the prairies were used to sharing as a community; individual farming did not conform to that practice. In addition, government-appointed Indian agents held all decision-making power on reserves.

First Nations groups were forced to learn a new way of life that was controlled by outsiders. Because the reserve system had broken up and isolated the various nations, there were few opportunities for group cooperation. The community was made less important than the individual, which was a denial of traditional First Nations culture.

Women's status

From 1951 onward, Indian women who married men without Indian status lost their own Indian status, until the law was repealed in 1985 by Bill C-31. They, along with their children, lost Indian status, the right to live in the reserve community, and the right to treaty benefits or to inherit reserve land from family members (Royal Commission on Aboriginal Peoples 1996a).

---

4. Reproduced with permission from Kainai Board of Education et al., *Peoples and Cultural Change: Aboriginal Studies 20* (Edmonton, AB: Duval House Publishing Inc., 2005), pp. 158, 161.

Aboriginal war veterans

Aboriginal Canadians enlisted in proportionately higher numbers during World War II than did any other segment of the general population. First Nations people had to choose between maintaining treaty status under the *Indian Act* or status as veterans. Most Aboriginal veterans were excluded from the standard veterans' benefits that should have been their right, such as the right to purchase or lease land under the *Veterans' Land Act*, and a grant or loan to start farming or a small business. Aboriginal veterans, including Métis and non-status Indians, had great difficulty obtaining dependents' allowance and other veterans' benefits to which they were entitled (Royal Commission on Aboriginal Peoples 1996a).

Right to vote

Registered First Nations people did not obtain the right to vote in federal elections until 1960, and the right to vote in Alberta provincial elections until 1965 (Royal Commission on Aboriginal Peoples 1996a).

Children in care

In 1959, only one percent of children in care of Social Services were of Aboriginal ancestry. By the end of the 1960s, 30 to 40 percent of children in care were Aboriginal, even though they only constituted four percent of Canada's population. In what is called the "Sixties Scoop" (which continued into the 1980s), these children were fostered or adopted out to predominantly white families. Many times, culturally valued ways of raising children were misinterpreted by social workers and this resulted in apprehension of the children.

Often moved from home to home, children in foster care suffered great losses, including loss of birth names and tribal identity, cultural identity and, for First Nations children, loss of Indian status (Fournier and Crey 1997).

Métis people

Métis are a distinct Aboriginal people with their own history, language and culture. The right to pursue a Métis way of life has been a long struggle. Throughout their history, Métis people endured repression, restrictions on trading, fraudulent schemes to dishonour Métis land entitlements, and marginalization of their culture and rights (Blackstock 2003).

In 1899, the Catholic missionary Father Albert Lacombe established an industrial residential school at St. Paul des Métis Settlement, in northeastern Alberta. In 1905, in response to the harsh discipline used to suppress Métis culture, traditions and values, students set the school on fire. It was never rebuilt.

In the late nineteenth century, pushed off their lands and unable to find work, many Métis people found themselves with nowhere to go. Looking for temporary shelter, they began to occupy small areas of land called road allowances. Road allowances were strips of land set aside by the Canadian government for future roads. They were usually on the edges of non-Aboriginal settlements or farms.[5]

Métis people would build shacks or log huts on these road allowances, with no guarantee that they would not be again displaced. They became known locally as the *road allowance people*.[5]

Despite the impermanence of the road allowance homes, some Métis people remember their lives there as living in strong community.[5]

The *Indian Act* often disregarded Métis heritage in its registration process. It was not until 1982 that Métis people were recognized in Section 35.2 of the Canadian Constitution, with "aboriginal peoples of Canada" defined as including the "Indian, Inuit and Métis peoples of Canada." It took until 2003 for the Supreme Court of Canada to rule that Métis people in and around Sault Ste. Marie were entitled to the same hunting and fishing rights as other Aboriginal peoples (CTV News, September 20, 2003).

In 1990, the Alberta government enacted legislation granting land title to the people of the Métis settlements. The legislation awarded Métis people title to 500 000 hectares of settlement land and $310 million payable over seventeen years. The money was for basic operations of the settlements and for economic development projects.[6]

The people of the Métis settlements finally have a voice in the administration of their lands and members of the settlements elect settlement councils.[6]

---

5. Adapted with permission from Kainai Board of Education et al., *Peoples and Cultural Change: Aboriginal Studies 20* (Edmonton, AB: Duval House Publishing Inc., 2005), p. 106.
6. Ibid., p. 127.

wisdom

Shared

> "To Métis people, the words *community* and *family* are almost interchangeable. Métis people view not only their relations as family, but friends, neighbours and workmates can all be a part of what a Métis person considers part of the family. In Métis culture, children are not solely the responsibility of their parents. The whole community traditionally shares in the task of raising the next generation. Elders, grandparents, aunts, uncles, trusted friends, leaders and other community members all have their vital role to play in shaping the future of our Nation."
>
> – Métis Family Services
> in Kainai Board of Education et al. 2005, p. 127

For more information about Aboriginal history

Kainai Board of Education, Métis Nation of Alberta, Northland School Division, Tribal Chiefs Institute of Treaty Six, Duval House Publishing and Alberta Education worked in partnership to develop a series of three student resources to support the Aboriginal Studies 10–20–30 program of studies. These award-winning resources are the first of their kind in Alberta and are a valuable reference for building an understanding of Aboriginal histories, cultures and perspectives.

Copies of these resources may be available at local libraries or can be purchased from the Learning Resources Centre at www.lrc.education.gov.ab.ca/ or at 780–427–2767.

To read more about:
- diverse cultural characteristics, origins, and migration and settlement patterns of Aboriginal peoples
- political and economic organization of Aboriginal peoples
- Aboriginal art forms, oral traditions and literature

see *Aboriginal Perspectives: Aboriginal Studies 10* (2004) by the Kainai Board of Education et al.

To read more about:
- Métis roles in the settlement of Western Canada
- effects of treaty relationships between First Nations peoples and the Government of Canada
- effects of government policies, legislation and practices on Aboriginal education, cultures and peoples

see *Peoples and Cultural Change: Aboriginal Studies 20* (2005) by the Kainai Board of Education et al.

To read more about:
- Aboriginal peoples' rights to self-government and self-determination
- Aboriginal land rights, entitlements and current land claim negotiations
- impact of colonialism experienced by Aboriginal peoples in Alberta
- common issues faced by indigenous peoples around the world

see *Contemporary Issues: Aboriginal Studies 30* (2005) by the Kainai Board of Education et al.

Diversity of Aboriginal Peoples

The term Aboriginal refers to the descendants of the original inhabitants of North America. The Canadian Constitution recognizes three groups of Aboriginal peoples: First Nations, Métis and Inuit.

Talking about Aboriginal cultures is equivalent to talking about Asian, European or African cultures—each of these cultures includes a wide variety of nations, customs, traditions, languages and outlooks. It would be misleading to suggest that a list of common cultural traits could describe the richness and diversity of Aboriginal cultures. With 44 First Nations, 8 Métis Settlements and many urban Aboriginal communities, Alberta's Aboriginal cultures are very diverse.

Culture as a framework[7]

Culture is the social framework for participating in and understanding the world. Every culture has key elements. The first is **worldview**—the way a group perceives and understands the world. The other four elements are the customs and routines that shape people's lives—an economy, a social structure, a form of government and a form of education. Generations transmit culture by immersing children in their particular version of these elements. Children learn their culture both formally (through deliberate teaching) and informally (through participating in the ways of their families and communities). As children grow up, they absorb the organization of life around them. They also absorb the way this organization changes. Sometimes it changes slowly, sometimes abruptly.

Abrupt change creates difficult transitions for cultures. During an abrupt change, key cultural elements can be lost between one generation and the next. Abrupt change can happen when crucial resources fail, when disease devastates families and communities. It can also happen when one culture overwhelms another, imposing new ideas and forms of education.

---

7. Reproduced with permission from Kainai Board of Education et al., *Peoples and Cultural Change: Aboriginal Studies 20* (Edmonton, AB: Duval House Publishing Inc., 2005), pp. 4, 5.

In Canada, Aboriginal peoples faced all of these forms of abrupt change, yet their cultures remain intact in many respects. As change swept over them, Aboriginal peoples thought about the future and secured their place in it. They also work for **cultural continuity** today, so that their communities can continue to evolve in their own way.

First Nations[8]

First Nations has more than one meaning. It often refers to a cultural group or nation of indigenous peoples, such as the Kainai, Cree, Anishinabé or Mi'kmaq. First Nations people were once known by the name *Indians*. However, *Indians* is considered offensive to many people today, partly because the name does not reflect the true position of First Nations as indigenous peoples of Canada. This resource uses names preferred by Aboriginal groups, unless quoting federal government legislation, where the term *Indian* is still common.

Canada's First Nations are diverse historically, culturally and linguistically. The term *First Nation* can also refer to the government of a group of First Nations people. There are over 630 First Nations governments today, each representing the interests of a distinct group of people.

Inuit peoples[8]

Inuit peoples are from Arctic areas of North America, as well as other countries with polar regions. *Inuit* means "the people" in Inuktitut, the Inuit language. Inuit peoples also have diverse cultural traits that vary across the huge Arctic region. Six variants of Inuktitut are spoken in Canada.

Inuit people are also indigenous to Canada, although they are culturally different from First Nations. Many of the Inuit people living in Alberta have moved here from the Arctic to pursue education or employment opportunities.

Métis people[8]

The term *métis* comes from a French word that refers to a person of mixed heritage. It first came into use in the sixteenth century, when the French began to visit North America regularly. Métis became a name used to describe the heritage of children born of French fur traders and First Nations women.

As the fur trade developed through the next 300 years, the name Métis gradually became more specific. Métis increasingly referred to a culturally distinct nation of people with First Nations-French ancestry.

---

8. Reproduced with permission from Kainai Board of Education et al., *Aboriginal Perspectives: Aboriginal Studies 10* (Edmonton, AB: Duval House Publishing Inc., 2005), pp. 4–5, 7.

Many of these people lived in the Red River area of what is now Manitoba.

In the twentieth century, the term became broader, often including people with an English- or Scottish-First Nations heritage who were also from Red River. Today political organizations such as the Métis Nation of Alberta define the Métis Nation as a group of individuals who are associated with a recognized Métis family or community and who self-identify as Métis people.

Linguistic groups[8]

Linguistic groups are sometimes useful in understanding cultural connections. A linguistic group is composed of nations who speak the same basic language, although different variations may exist. For example, the Cree linguistic group has five major variants across Canada. One Cree person speaking to another in a different variant could likely make himself or herself understood. However, a Cree person speaking to a Blackfoot speaker will not be understood, even though Cree and Blackfoot are part of the same language family. Blackfoot is its own linguistic group.

Individual communities within one linguistic group can also show many cultural differences from one another.

For more information, see *Appendix 1: Treaty Area Map of Alberta, Appendix 2: First Nations and First Nations Communities in Alberta, Appendix 3: Métis Settlements and Regional Zones in Alberta* and *Appendix 4: First Nations and Métis Language Groups in Alberta.*

Common threads

Although common threads may run through the experiences of Aboriginal students, each student will bring a varying degree of involvement with aspects of traditional and contemporary Aboriginal cultures and mainstream cultures. Aboriginal students at post-secondary institutions in Alberta represent about 70 different Aboriginal cultures and societies. This cultural diversity among Aboriginal students is particularly evident in urban centres.

Aboriginal students:
- may identify themselves as First Nations, Métis or Inuit—or they may not identify themselves as Aboriginal at all
- may live a traditional, bicultural or assimilated lifestyle
- may have an urban, rural, reserve or settlement background
- may speak an Aboriginal language at home, or may hear and understand an Aboriginal language but not be able to speak it.

Learning about students' cultures helps teachers better support their success. It is important for teachers to take the time to listen to Aboriginal students and families, and learn about their unique histories and cultures.

about Aboriginal people

Statistics

From 1996 to 2001, the Aboriginal population grew by more than 22 percent while the non-Aboriginal population increased by only 3.4 percent (CBC News in Review, 2003).

The median age of Aboriginal peoples is well below that of the non-Aboriginal population. In 2001, 50 percent of the First Nations population was less than 24.7 years (Statistics Canada, 2001 Census).

The number of Registered Indians in Alberta is projected to increase from 87,311 in 2000 to 128,103 by the year 2021 (Indian and Northern Affairs Canada, and Statistics Canada n.d.).

Twenty-five percent of the Aboriginal population lives in 10 urban centres—Winnipeg has the greatest number, followed by Edmonton, Vancouver and Calgary (Statistics Canada, 2001 Census).

For a *Glossary of Terms* related to Aboriginal history and diversity, see page 151.

Worldviews and Education

Each Aboriginal group expresses its culture in various ways—a result of geographic circumstances and each group's unique history. At the same time, many Aboriginal peoples throughout North America share similar guiding thoughts and traditional values.

These common threads running through many Aboriginal cultures are sometimes referred to as foundational worldviews. They reflect the guiding principles and traditional values of Aboriginal societies. They suggest the way Aboriginal peoples see themselves in relation to the world.

Traditional Aboriginal education is based upon these worldviews—it is a holistic process where learning takes place across different spheres of human experience including spiritual, physical, emotional and mental dimensions. Worldviews may also consider relationships and experiences of the past, present and future as interconnected.

13

Spirituality, relationships and the expression of traditional values are the heart of Aboriginal education. Each sphere needs to be addressed in each subject area. Spiritual, physical, emotional and mental spheres should be considered within each learning activity. For example, a Grade 1 science unit on colour could move beyond simply identifying colours to exploring how colours have special significance in symbols, dress and natural objects. This is in contrast to Western education, where these dimensions tend to be addressed more in isolation—for example, the physical sphere is addressed in physical education and the spiritual sphere is addressed in religion or not at all.

In a contemporary setting, Aboriginal education is what happens when attitudes, approaches and actions allow Aboriginal students to become fully participating co-creators of society. Aboriginal education recognizes the significant and valuable contributions—past, present and future—of Aboriginal people to society.

Shared wisdom

Traditional values
"A holistic philosophy and psychology rooted in traditional Native values can improve the educational opportunities for Native children."

– Joe Couture, Cree Elder

Effective education that includes Aboriginal worldviews does not exclude or discredit other cultures but ensures that non-Aboriginal students and Aboriginal students alike are given the opportunity to see Aboriginal perspectives, and the strengths and gifts of Aboriginal people reflected in the schools they attend.

There are five strong threads common to Aboriginal worldviews that can be brought to life in the classroom:
- a holistic perspective
- the interconnectedness of all living things
- connection to the land and community
- the dynamic nature of the world
- strength in "power with."

A holistic perspective
While Western education often focuses on verbal thinking and uses an analytical approach to learning, Aboriginal worldviews address the whole person, encompassing their mental, physical, emotional and spiritual capabilities in relation to all living things.

Aboriginal worldviews assume that all forms are interconnected, that the survival of each life form is dependent on the survival of all others. Aboriginal worldviews also note that the force that animates the life forms is derived from an unseen but knowable spiritual realm.

Aboriginal worldviews see a unified vision, rather than an artificial fragmentation of concepts. These worldviews assert that all life is sacred and that all life forms are connected. Humans are neither above nor below others in the circle of life. Everything that exists in the circle is one unity, one heart.

Western education often artificially separates learning into discrete subject areas. An Aboriginal perspective uses an integrated approach. For example, the making of a star quilt would be seen as an art involving geometry (including symmetry and rotations), an opportunity to meet a quilt maker from the community, and a way to learn cultural teachings regarding the star pattern and quilt. Quiltmaking is often a communal experience and this working with others to meet a common goal is an opportunity to explore and learn about the importance of establishing and maintaining relationships.

Consider the following strategies for fostering this perspective.

- Build learning activities around meaningful content that relates to students' experiences and engages them in tasks based on their learning interests.

- Allow opportunities for visual symbolic thinking and holistic, rather than analytical, approaches to education.

- Look for opportunities to make connections among subject areas, for example, social studies, literature and art.

- Explore the ways in which learning can happen as a result of flexible scheduling. For example, can scheduling changes on a field trip accommodate opportunities for holistic learning?

- When appropriate, ask a member of the Aboriginal community to assist with the learning and to provide an Aboriginal perspective. This will enhance the credibility of the learning activity, and build a connection between the school and the community.

wisdom

Shared

> **Web of life**
> "All things and all people, though we have our own individual gifts and special place, are dependent on and share in the growth and work of everything and everyone else. We believe that beings thrive when there is a web of interconnectedness between the individual and the community, and between the community and nature.
>
> Everything we do, every decision we make, affects our family, our community, it affects the air we breathe, the animals, the plants, the water in some way. Each of us is totally dependent on everything else."
>
> – Evelyn Steinhauer

The interconnectedness of all living things

Aboriginal worldviews recognize the interconnectedness of all living things and the spirit that exists within each. Spirituality, personal health, community health and the health of the environment are understood to be interrelated.

With the recognition of the connections among all things come the questions—What are an individual's relations to other people? To nature? To the land?

All individuals assume a responsibility for themselves, not in isolation, but in relation to all else. Each individual is regarded as a participating, contributing member of the group. Cooperation and sharing are vital.

Consider the following strategies for fostering this perspective.

- Create a classroom community. Encourage each student to be a contributor.

- Encourage students to be aware of their sphere of influence and to always consider the impact of their actions on others and on the classroom community.

Connection to the land and community

A sacred relationship with nature is the heart of traditional teachings and practices. From the understanding of the interconnectedness of all things comes the understanding that the well-being of the Earth is essential for survival.

16

Growing out of this connection to the Earth, Aboriginal worldviews encompass a fluid sense of time and the cyclical nature of change—day and night, the seasons, life and death.

Connection to the Earth also teaches about the importance of place and of the connection to a place of belonging. The Earth provides the land on which people build communities—land and community dictate a way of life.

Consider the following strategies for fostering this perspective.

- Explore ways to create a sense of home in the classroom and school for Aboriginal students and families. Think about how to draw people into the classroom and make them feel welcome.

- Recognize and celebrate the seasons and the changes that they bring. Use nature as a classroom. Mark occasions. This tends to be more challenging at the senior high school level where bigger, less personal surroundings and the pressures of curriculum content mean that rather than celebrating the seasons, for example, the year is marked by mid-terms and finals.

- Create opportunities for experiential learning. For example, when teaching students about traditional Aboriginal food such as blueberries, plan the learning activity so that the class can go out to the land and actually have the experience of picking berries.

The dynamic nature of the world
Aboriginal cultures are dynamic, adaptive and adapting, not limited to the past.

In Aboriginal worldviews, everything—people, relationships, situations—is dynamic. Individuals change, and Aboriginal cultures evolve and adapt. Learning is recognized as a creative process from which new structures, forms and practices evolve.

Considering the following strategies for fostering this perspective.

- Encourage students to consider multiple perspectives. Focus less on opinion and argument or right and wrong, and encourage students to share and extend their own thinking through discussion with others.

- Explore the relationships between concepts. Encourage students to go beyond dichotomous "this OR that" thinking. Help them focus on multiple possibilities instead—"this AND that."

- Be aware that Aboriginal languages tend to be more descriptive and more action-oriented than English. Aboriginal languages tend to describe concepts such as snow and wind by what and how they do something, whereas English simply tends to name the concept.

Strength in "power with"

In Aboriginal cultures, worldviews reflect "power with," rather than "power over." The image for this concept is a circle, and all living things are viewed as equal within the circle. "Power with" is a dialogue, where everyone stands on the ground, face to face.

The image for "power over" is a pyramid, with those at the top holding the greatest power. "Power over" is a hierarchy, where the few stand above the many.

Consider the following strategies to reflect "power with" in the classroom.

- Learn from the students about how they learn best. Work in genuine collaboration with them to determine the approaches that are most effective.

- Involve students when making decisions about the classroom. Provide opportunities for developing their skills so that they become effective at making *real* decisions about things that matter. Work toward consensus.

- Invite older or stronger students to mentor younger or less able students. Find ways to reverse the process, e.g., find a skill that a younger student could mentor in an older student.

- Welcome and validate parent input into decision making about their child's education. Treat them as full partners in the collaboration that is essential for supporting their child's learning.

- Recognize that parents have expert knowledge about their Aboriginal community. Ask for their help and advice in choosing classroom visitors, and connecting with other community and cultural resources.

Cultural Continuity

"Aboriginal people often say, 'Our children are our future.' By extension, then, the future depends on the effectiveness of education. Education shapes the pathways of thinking, transmits values as well as facts, teaches language and social skills, helps release creative potential and determines productive capacities" (Royal Commission on Aboriginal Peoples 1996a, p. 82).

In support of Aboriginal education, Alberta Learning published its comprehensive First Nations, Métis and Inuit report in 2002. Its goals include:

- high quality learning opportunities that are responsive, flexible, accessible and affordable to the learner
- excellence in learner achievement.

wisdom

Shared

> **Living culture**
> "The objective of Aboriginal education is to develop knowledge, skills and values rooted in the centuries old tradition.
>
> We must always remember that culture is something that does not keep still; it develops through challenges and interactions of people and events or it becomes distorted and dies. It is the continuity of living culture that is important …".
>
> – Joe Couture, Cree Elder

Schools and teachers across the province are encouraged to provide culturally appropriate education for their Aboriginal students. Students report that their most positive learning experiences involve times when culture is reflected in the classroom or when there is a strong relationship of respect and encouragement with an educator.

Overall, Aboriginal people want two basic things from the education system. They want schools to help children, youth and adults learn the skills they need to participate fully in the economy. And they want schools to help children and youth develop as citizens of Aboriginal nations—with the knowledge of their histories, languages and traditions necessary for cultural continuity (Royal Commission on Aboriginal Peoples 1996a).

Regardless of their heritage, students learn best when they learn in context—when they can relate what they are learning to their own experience. In this sense, Aboriginal students are often at a disadvantage because many aspects of Aboriginal culture are not reflected in their classrooms.

To work effectively with Aboriginal students, teachers need to realize how vital cultural continuity is to student achievement.

What does cultural continuity mean?

It is the process of integrating culture into students' daily learning, a process that encourages students to learn from a position of wholeness, where they can see their reality and experiences reflected in what is being learned and how it is being taught.

Cultural continuity threads through both content and process in the classroom. It involves culture in its broadest and deepest sense—it includes the worldviews and traditional values of Aboriginal peoples. These are expressed in history, religion, laws, the arts, patterns of communication, decision making, and relationships among individuals and groups—and all other aspects of human interaction and endeavour.

Shared wisdom

Recapturing our wholeness

"… if we go back to the origin of the word heal … it is structurally related to the word whole, which is in itself related to the word holy. And this is something I understand we are all trying to do together. The healing process is a way of recapturing our wholeness.

… I would suggest, not only to Native people, but to many people both in Canada and the United States, there has been a history of people being told to amputate a part of themselves to be able to fit something that's rigid and not built for them in the first place. Amputate … your language, your spirituality, whatever, as Bateson would say, is a difference that makes a difference … Part of what we are going to do now is a healing process in the sense of reclaiming wholeness.

… what we are doing here is a sacred thing, and I cannot emphasize that enough. It is not about academic credits, and it is not about certifications. It is a sacred work to reclaim wholeness."

– Tafoya 1995, p. 27

Learning About Cultural Differences

Becoming more familiar with students' cultural backgrounds will help teachers:
- understand how cultural differences may affect students' learning
- understand students' motivations and values
- adapt materials and approaches appropriately
- build mutual respect.

wisdom

Shared

Cultural awareness
"Only after we become aware of the [cultural] differences and understand them well enough to accept them as equally valid and good are we prepared to teach these students. Then neither the teacher nor the child will be pressured to adopt the other's culture, and mutual respect and understanding can develop."

– Gilliland 1999, p. 5

An effective way of learning about students' Aboriginal cultures is for teachers to become aware of their own perspectives, for example, to reflect on what they know about Aboriginal cultures and how they have learned what they know.

wisdom

Shared

Cultural perspectives
"Our perceptions of the ways others think and act depend on our cultural perspective, which depends, in part, on our understanding that cultural differences *do* exist among groups. Equally important is the ability to recognize the vast diversity *within* cultural groups. Without such a recognition, we run the risk of stereotyping people."

– Chamberlain 2005, p. 197

Not understanding cross-cultural differences can hamper teachers' effectiveness. The following six fundamental patterns of cultural differences—ways in which cultures tend to vary from one another—are a framework that teachers can use to build their own understanding and appreciation of cross-cultural differences. This framework includes communication styles, attitudes towards conflict, approaches to completing tasks, decision-making styles, attitudes towards openness in personal matters and different approaches to knowing.

Communication styles
Consider language use (for example, how many meanings does the word "yes" have, depending on how you say it) and nonverbal communication.

Within different Aboriginal communities, individuals may verbally or nonverbally acknowledge what is said, for example, by nodding or saying "yes" or "ummhmm." This may simply be recognition of a person's right to speak and to share ideas or opinions. It does not necessarily signal agreement with the idea or opinion.

Attitudes towards conflict

In some cultures, conflict is seen as a positive opportunity to work out differences, while in others it is something to be avoided because it is demeaning or embarrassing.

Survival in small traditional Aboriginal communities depended, in part, on the ability of their members to work together. In many Aboriginal cultures, direct confrontation was avoided in order to maintain cooperative relations. Instead, a more indirect approach was often taken, for example, by telling an individual a story with a lesson.

Similarly, students and families in the school may not be comfortable with conflict or addressing issues that will focus attention on them. Teachers report that their Aboriginal students may avoid conflict by quietly leaving the school or the community for a time.

Approaches to completing tasks

Approaches to tasks vary from culture to culture. In some cultures, people get to know each other through the work rather than taking time to establish relationships before the work begins. Different concepts of time may affect task completion.

In Aboriginal communities, individuals tend to take the time to greet each other and establish a relationship before they begin to work. This time of establishing a relationship is considered a necessary part of addressing the task. Different communities have different protocols for introductions and approaching others, gathering information, and working with others. It is important to ask about and follow the established protocol for the community.

Traditional Aboriginal education emphasizes contextual and meaningful learning. Thus, educational activities need to be relevant to the daily activities of the students. If they do not see a clear and immediate connection to their world, then it is likely that other activities will take precedence over schoolwork.

By taking the time to establish a strong relationship with students, teachers increase the likelihood students will give higher priority to the tasks teachers assign.

Decision-making styles

In some cultures, decisions are made by a leader; in others, they are made by delegation or by consensus.

In many Aboriginal families, decisions are made collaboratively rather than by one individual. This allows everyone who is affected by the decision to have opportunity for input. Rather than making decisions on the spot, time is often taken for reflection.

Women play an important role in making key decisions. In many traditional Aboriginal societies, women were engaged in prominent leadership roles. They participated actively in political and cultural life, either publicly or behind the scenes. They had considerable influence on family affairs, especially as they grew older and were seen as women of wisdom. Although colonialism disrupted cultural practices and introduced discrimination against women, Aboriginal women are once again becoming an increasingly strong voice on both the political and home fronts.

When making decisions or solving problems, Aboriginal parents and students may consult with supportive family or community members.

Reflecting this collaborative approach, decisions about student learning should be made using a consensus model, with parents and students as key partners in the process.

Attitudes towards openness in personal matters

In some cultural groups, it is appropriate to be open about emotions, about reasons behind a conflict and about personal information, as a way of building trust. In other cultures, trust must be developed before personal information can be shared. People's degree of openness in personal matters will vary from community to community and from individual to individual.

Developing a relationship built on trust and acceptance is paramount when working with Aboriginal students and families. Knowing and respecting the situations faced by many Aboriginal students and families will go a long way in developing this trust. When trust is established, students and their families will relate in a more meaningful and personal way with teachers and other school personnel.

Different approaches to knowing

Cultural groups may differ in the way in which information is gathered, for example, through objective means, through imagery or through inner knowing.

23

Mainstream education systems tend to validate knowledge gained through objective means, such as quantitative research or tested hypotheses. Credentials and "book knowledge" tend to be placed in high regard.

In traditional Aboriginal education systems, learning is seen as an individual's lifelong responsibility. Traditional teachings stress personal responsibility and relationships. Teachers model competent and respectful behaviour. A specific product or grade is not as important as the process of learning and living.[9]

wisdom

Shared

"We had ... our own teachings, our own education system – teaching children that way of life was taught [by] the grandparents and extended families; they were taught how to view and respect the land and everything in Creation.

Through that, the young people were [educated about] what were the Creator's laws, what were these natural laws. What were these First Nations' laws. And talk revolved around a way of life, based on their values. For example: ... to share, to care, to be respectful of people, how to help oneself. How to help others. How to work together ..."

– Peter Waskahat, Cree Elder, Frog Lake First Nation
in Cardinal and Hildebrandt 2000, pp. 15–16

The holistic nature of traditional education shapes the teaching styles and methods. This educational philosophy nurtures learners, showing them how to achieve their individual goals while at the same time meeting the collective needs of the community. Education passes on the values central to Aboriginal communities and families.[9]

Traditional Aboriginal education prepares students for total living. It focuses on a multidimensional approach balanced to meet the emotional, mental, physical and spiritual needs of the learner.[9]

Teachers concentrate on what learners can do rather than what they cannot. This reinforces each learner's unique abilities. Traditional teaching strategies involve:
- strong visual components or tools
- learning in real life, rather than by practice in artificial settings
- a focus on people and relationships rather than on information.[9]

9. Reproduced with permission from Kainai Board of Education et al., *Peoples and Cultural Change: Aboriginal Studies 20* (Edmonton, AB: Duval House Publishing Inc., 2005), p. 173.

In Aboriginal cultures, knowledge is often embedded within the language of the community. Information tends to be framed around relationships such as the interconnectedness of humans, animals, plants, the environment and the Creator. Information is gathered and shared holistically. The oral tradition is used to ensure knowledge is shared from generation to generation.

stories

Shared

> "Traditionally, Aboriginal cultural knowledge is transmitted and documented primarily through the oral tradition, but also through such things as dramatic productions, dance performances, and they are documented on such artifacts as wampum belts, birch bark scrolls, totem poles, petroglyphs and masks. This is the Aboriginal way of transmitting knowledge and of recording information and history."
>
> – Greg Young-Ing
> in Royal Commission on Aboriginal Peoples 1996c, p. 591

At the core of traditional education lies Aboriginal spirituality and traditional knowledge. Elders play a vital role passing on traditional knowledge to students. Holistic teachings and counselling from Elders brings continuity to students' lives—they learn from Elders both in and out of school. By conducting and providing instruction in ceremonies such as Sweat Lodges and pipe ceremonies, Elders teach learners to honour what is sacred in the universe as well as what is sacred in themselves. These ceremonies are powerful tools that can show learners that they are integral, respected members of their community.[10] Adhering to ceremonial protocols can also help individuals build self-discipline, and strengthen their relationships with others and with the physical and spiritual world around them.

Like all peoples, Aboriginal peoples rely on education to continue their culture. Using extensive parental and community participation, Aboriginal educators work toward developing qualities and values in their students that include respect for Elders, cultural tradition, leadership, generosity, integrity, wisdom, compassion for others and living in harmony with the environment.[10]

---

10. Reproduced with permission from Kainai Board of Education et al., *Peoples and Cultural Change: Aboriginal Studies 20* (Edmonton, AB: Duval House Publishing Inc., 2005), p. 173.

Getting Started: Learning and Teaching About Aboriginal Cultures

The more teachers know about the histories, languages and cultures of Aboriginal peoples, the more comfortable they are using the range of resources and materials available to help them. Consider the following strategies for learning and teaching about Aboriginal cultures.

Start with students

Students may have a wealth of information. Approach them discreetly, as many Aboriginal students do not want to be singled out as being different in front of their classmates. Ask them what they know about language and culture. Ask them who they know in the community. They may be able to suggest people that teachers can talk with or invite into the class.

Get to know parents

Encourage parents to visit the classroom. Follow-up on invitations to visit with them at home or in the community, for example, at a round dance or pow-wow. Ask them for suggestions about classroom visitors and for introductions to individuals and organizations in the community.

Contact appropriate organizations

Find out if the school jurisdiction or a neighbouring jurisdiction has Aboriginal consultants or liaison workers, and get to know them. Most post-secondary institutions in Alberta have liaison workers who are aware of community events and resources for Aboriginal people. Friendship Centres can put teachers in touch with individuals who can visit classrooms and they are also a good source for information about community events and resources.

Look for resources

Teachers can use print resources, Web sites, videos and other sources of information to increase their own cultural awareness and to build cultural continuity in the curriculum they teach. Parents and other community members can provide excellent feedback regarding the appropriateness and cultural validity of resources for use in the classroom.

Learn about contemporary issues in the Aboriginal community

Follow the stories in the mainstream media but dig deeper. Read an Aboriginal newspaper. Visit the Web site of an Aboriginal organization.

Be willing to invest time

Realize that it will take time to learn about the community and to build relationships. When people recognize that a teacher is sincere, open and respectful, most people will value that teacher's interest and effort.

Participate in professional development opportunities

Look for opportunities for ongoing multidimensional professional development that will help build an understanding of contemporary issues that affect First Nations, Métis and Inuit learners and explore thinking strategies that will best meet the needs of these students.

Chapter 2

Aboriginal Students:
Who are they? How do they learn?

The information and stories in this chapter will help teachers to:
- recognize Aboriginal students as individual learners within a cultural context
- become more aware of how the influences of family, culture and language affect the learning strengths and needs of each student
- use a strength-seeking approach to assess students' needs
- collaborate in an ongoing relationship with each student to meet the student's learning needs and support the student's learning strengths.

In Aboriginal worldviews, each individual is unique and has the ability to fully actualize or to become whole. This understanding accepts that each student can learn—the question is how does each student learn best?

The teacher's role is to facilitate this learning process, to unlock each student's potential. The best way for the teacher to help students do this is to come to know them as individual learners within their cultural context. It is important for teachers to:
- learn about the ways that students reflect the Aboriginal worldviews and cultures of their families and communities
- learn about how students learn so that teachers can adjust classroom practices to facilitate learning
- promote mastery learning by teaching students to learn about how they learn (metacognition) and to use their unique learning processes to master the curriculum.

Shared wisdom

Importance of relationship
"Teachers need to learn how to unpack the nature of the relationship between themselves and their students so that both know how the patterns they are used to are either complementary or may be in conflict with each other's patterns … Only when both feel they have an investment in the outcome of the relationship can gains be made towards meeting each other's desire for success."

– Wilson 2001

It is difficult to fully understand how worldviews and cultures influence students, because they thread through every aspect of the learning process. There is a great deal for teachers to learn.

It is worthwhile to be patient. Elders place much hope in the education system and in teachers' abilities to help Aboriginal children. Aboriginal communities have high standards for their children's education. They not only want their children to do well, they want quality learning opportunities for their community. The time teachers spend getting to know the students and their patterns of learning provides the foundation for a strong learning relationship.

Learning About Students: Family, Cultural Identity and Language

In the holistic worldviews of Aboriginal communities, a teacher is teaching not only the child who comes to school but also the child who is a member of a family, a community and a culture. It is important to learn about each student as an individual. In this way, teachers begin to find out about the cultural uniqueness of their Aboriginal students rather than relying on preconceived notions about students, their families and their communities.

Although the need to establish a relationship may seem self-evident, with Aboriginal students this is a vital step that connects to culture, where all learning is based, first of all, on relationship. Offering kindness, trust and a positive awareness of family and culture sets the stage for students to feel welcome and to want to attend school every day.

Some Aboriginal students enter the classroom looking and acting very much like other students—wearing the same clothes, using similar language and displaying similar attitudes. Some Aboriginal students may even be blonde, blue-eyed and fair in complexion. Other Aboriginal students may look and/or act differently than other students.

Despite outward appearances, the strongest influences on both groups of students are likely to be those influences that cannot be seen—the influences of their histories, families and cultures. To understand this is to understand the context of the classroom within the community. These influences may run so deep that even the students themselves are not fully aware of them and may not be able to explain how they affect them.

The more teachers know about each of these elements in their students' lives, the more information they have to create an understanding of their students' lives.

Family

Family is the place where children begin their learning. Like all students, Aboriginal students' experiences of school will be significantly affected by their family life. Though each family is unique and family contexts may range from highly traditional to virtually assimilated, the following threads may run through the family experiences of many students.

- Many Aboriginal students have a large extended family. Their "close" relatives may include people who in other cultures may be considered "distant" relatives.

- It is common practice for adults other than the students' parents—grandparents, aunts, uncles, cousins, older siblings—to take on the role of the adults involved with the school.

- Sixty-five percent of Aboriginal children on reserve and 50 percent of children in urban settings live with two parents. In comparison, 83 percent of non-Aboriginal children live with two parents (Statistics Canada, 2001 Census).

- Because of cultural disruption and misunderstanding between cultures, about 5 percent of Aboriginal children living in urban areas no longer live with their parents, but live with other relatives or nonrelatives, compared to 0.6 percent of non-Aboriginal children (Statistics Canada, 2001 Census). Many of these children are in foster care.

- A growing number of Aboriginal families live in urban settings. Many parents and older students move from a reserve or small community to an urban centre for work or education, leaving their extended families behind. Moving often means leaving behind the friends and family that support them and adapting to a different way of life.

- Family events and gatherings are very important—students may be out of school for several days at a time to attend them.

- Aboriginal families often use a nondirective approach to guiding their children. This arises out of worldviews that respect everyone's right to make his or her own decisions. This noninterference may sometimes be mistaken for a lack of concern or permissiveness. However, it is quite the opposite—it is a deliberate parenting approach that expects children to mature and determine their own actions from an early age. Noninterference also reflects a preference for experiential learning.

wisdom

Shared

> **On noninterference**
> "Spiritual being essentially requires only that individuals seek their place in the universe; everything else will follow in good time … Because everything was created with a specific purpose to fulfill, no one should have the power to interfere or to impose upon others which path is the best to follow."
>
> – Garrett et al. 2003, p. 229

- Older siblings may be required to help out at home and often take care of younger children. This may affect their ability to take part in extracurricular activities, and to complete homework and assignments on time.

- The heart of traditional Aboriginal learning is experiential. Aboriginal cultures were built on oral traditions. As a result of the influence of these oral traditions, many students' parents and grandparents have little reading material in their homes. Because of this, some Aboriginal students may have had less early experience with reading than students from other cultures and may view reading as being less important.

Learning about family and culture helps teachers to:
- recognize the cultural influences that affect learning
- draw attention to positive values in the students' cultures
- make meaningful connections between Aboriginal cultures and the curriculum
- detect and counter stereotypes
- build on students' strengths.

Cultural identity

In a mainstream setting, when people meet for the first time, they will probably ask each other who they are and what they do. In Aboriginal communities, people tend to ask people who they are, who their family is and where they are from. The answers to these questions say much about each person's languages, traditions and customs, and help to create relationship.

How will a teacher know which students in the class are Aboriginal? Skin, hair and eye colour will not establish identity and in many cases, neither will family names. The best way for teachers to learn about students' backgrounds is to share stories and information about themselves first. This provides a model for the student. Then, when opportunities arise, the teacher can invite students to share information about themselves and their cultures. Often students will be more comfortable doing this in a one-to-one situation, rather than in a large group. Consider the following kinds of questions to explore with students.

- Are they First Nations, Métis, Inuit? How do they identify themselves?

- Do they speak an Aboriginal language? Do their parents or grandparents?

- What are the special events in their community—for example, rodeos, pow-wows or fiddling competitions?

- What do they know about their histories and cultures, and are they interested in learning more?

- How do they describe their families?

Respect that not all students want to be identified as Aboriginal in front of their peers. Through the process of colonization, many Aboriginal people learned to be ashamed of their cultural identity and so students may claim to belong to another ethnic group instead. These students still benefit from the cultural awareness and respect that teachers establish in their classrooms. They may begin to claim their identity as they learn that it is safe to do so in the classroom environment.

wisdom

Shared

Take time
"When you take the time to talk to students, remember: the first moments are sacred; they involve the honouring of the dignity of each life that you meet. Take the time to listen with your heart."

– Aboriginal teacher

Preservation of languages

Many Aboriginal people in Alberta are concerned about the increasing decline in knowledge of Aboriginal languages. About 25 percent of Aboriginal people in Canada can carry on a conversation in an Aboriginal language. Reported use of Cree, Ojibway and Blackfoot declined between 1996 and 2001 (Statistics Canada, 2001 Census). Language vitality is maintained only through regular use.

Alberta Education is working to promote cultures and languages in Alberta's schools. Blackfoot and Cree 10, 20, 30 courses are currently being taught in a number of Alberta senior high schools. Junior high learning resources for both Blackfoot and Plains Cree have been developed in cooperation with First Nations education authorities (e.g., the Kainai Board from the Blood reserve and Treaty 6 Tribal Ventures).

In addition, Alberta Education and the Alexis Board of Education are developing Stoney/Nakoda language courses.

Influence of language

Because of the way it shapes their thinking—their ways of knowing—many Aboriginal people say culture *is* their language. Language patterns are deeply woven into the lives of Aboriginal students, their families and their communities, regardless of their fluency in an Aboriginal language. In fact, language patterns tend to endure for three generations—a student whose great-grandparents were the most recent Aboriginal language speakers in the family will still be influenced by their language patterns.

The first language of some students is an Aboriginal language. As they speak English, these students are constantly translating their thoughts. This process may be difficult as the meaning of the words and the patterns of thinking in their first language may be quite different from English.

Shared **wisdom**

"The simplicity of our daily life does not indicate that our vocabulary is simple and limited to a few hard-to-gurgle grunts. It is true that we have some tongue twisters, which only go to show that the Cree tongue is highly developed. We have every reason to believe that ours is a beautiful language and so expressive and descriptive …

For illustration let us take the word "snow." … whereas the Cree word for snow is *kona*, while for snowing we have *mispon*, melting snow *sasken*, drifting snow *piwon*, and snow drifts *papestin*. … we do not attach other words to *kona* for every new word that relates to snow."

– Dion 1979, p. 2

For speakers of an Aboriginal language, English can seem very linear and lacking in context. It is important to give students time to articulate their thoughts and to find ways to help them express themselves clearly and comfortably.

It is also important to be aware of tone, volume and pitch. Speakers of Aboriginal languages often speak in softer tones. They listen carefully to voice inflection and so may be very sensitive not only to what is being said but *how* it is being said. Aboriginal people often use humour—there is a lot of laughter in Aboriginal conversations.

The languages of students' Aboriginal communities may have a strong influence on their thought and speech patterns, even if the students do not speak the language. For example, people from different cultural backgrounds vary in their "pause times" (the time before replying) in a conversation. The pause time for European people tends to be less than two seconds. The pause time for Aboriginal peoples tends to be about four or five seconds.

Because of this, Aboriginal students may find it difficult to take part in class discussions where, typically, students jump into the conversation as soon as the previous speaker has finished.

To accommodate the learning needs of Aboriginal students, teachers can increase "wait time"—the thinking time they give students after asking a question and before expecting a response. Generous wait time has been shown to increase the length and quality of student responses.

wisdom

Shared

Wait time
"Indigenous pedagogy accepts students' cognitive search for learning processes they can internalize, and Aboriginal teachers allow for a lag period of watching before doing."

– Battiste 2002, pp. 18–19

Working from Strength

When assessing the learning needs and preferences of Aboriginal students, especially those who may be struggling with school, one effective approach is to recognize and build on their strengths. Positive models, such as the Positive Youth Development approach (Seita and Brendtro 2002), identify the ways in which students cope successfully in a variety of situations, including a range of strengths that may not typically show themselves in the classroom setting.

Positive approaches do not ignore student needs and challenges. Rather, they provide a balance to assessment models that tend to focus on student deficits rather than potential.

The Positive Youth Development approach uses the four principles of connections, continuity, dignity and opportunity as a framework for assessment that emphasizes strengths.

Connections

- Who are the significant people in a student's life?
- What are the student's relationships with family, friends and community?
- Who does the student rely on for support?
- What people strengths does the student have?

Continuity

- What life challenges does the student face?
- How is the student coping with these challenges?
- What difficulties has the student overcome?
- How does the student ask for help with these challenges?
- Who does the student ask for help?
- How can the student be helped with these life challenges?

Dignity

- How does the student feel about himself or herself?
- What are the student's hopes and dreams?
- Does the student feel in control of his or her life?
- How does the student treat others?
- How can the student be supported in developing self-respect and strength?

Opportunity

How can the student be supported in developing:

- a sense of belonging
- a sense of mastery
- a sense of responsibility and independence
- a sense of sharing, generosity and compassion?

These four principles are a blueprint for strength-seeking instead of flaw-fixing interventions. The goal is to create environments where all students can thrive and grow.

Helping Students Learn About Learning

Thinking about thinking and learning about learning—or metacognition—is fundamental to working with Aboriginal students. The more students can recognize and articulate which learning processes and preferences work best for them, and in which situations, the easier it will be for them to learn and for teachers to support their learning.

The process of helping students learn about their learning is:

- a collaboration—teacher and student work together in a relationship
- an ongoing dialogue—talking about learning becomes part of classroom routine, one-on-one, in groups and as a class
- based on observation and listening—the student is the best teacher when it comes to his or her abilities and learning needs.

In this process, reflection becomes a key part of every learning activity. Teachers can expect these reflections to become more detailed and complex as the school year progresses. The more students learn about learning, the better able they are to meet their own learning challenges, to teach other students about *their* learning and to teach other teachers. They take more ownership of their own learning.

This mastery becomes increasingly important as students move through grade levels and on to different classrooms and schools, where they will need strong self-advocacy skills in order to succeed.

Teacher story

Learning by watching

"I invited a traditional teacher to teach the class about tipis. His approach was really interesting. He demonstrated how to put up the tipi, and then put them to work in groups, setting up model tipis. He didn't guide them verbally, he just observed them. When he saw that students were having trouble, he had them watch his demonstration again. He let them learn by doing—it seemed like he never doubted they'd be able to do it, and he was right. And the students were happy because they accomplished this on their own. Thinking about experiential learning and how much students really do learn by observation—this seems like an approach I'd like to try myself."

Learning preferences

"In Aboriginal thought a whole person consists of spirit, heart, mind and body—the capacity to see, feel, know and do. Therefore, in the learning process, a whole person engages his or her physical, mental, emotional and spiritual capacities in receiving data or information for the brain to process" (Hill 1999, p. 100).

There is no "learning style unique to Aboriginal learners." When students understand how they receive information and process it—when they identify their learning preferences—they increase their ability to take control of their own learning processes.

37

Teacher story

How students like to learn

A master teacher we know uses a comment box to find out about her students' experiences. Here are some comments she gathered when she asked her students how they like to learn.

"I learn by doing."
"When I study, I like to chew gum and play with a keychain or elastic band or something."
"I learn by reading and highlighting what I've read."
"I like to build things and work with my hands."
"I learn by reading and then repeating it out loud."
"I learn by working slowly and by understanding the problem."
"I listen to music while I do homework or study."
"I learn by working with other people."
"I learn by observing and observing other people learning."
"I listen best in class when I'm doodling or drawing something."
"I learn by viewing, tasting, listening, hearing, all of the senses."

The teacher's comment when she read these responses?

"Each student clearly learned in a unique way. I thought back on the number of times I limited learning by determining the learning process."

Aboriginal educator Diane Hill uses a circle to illustrate the four elements involved in the learning process cycle: to see, to feel, to know and to do.[11] Each type of learner has a place within the circle. Whether the students learn best by seeing, feeling, knowing or doing indicates whether they are intuitive, emotional-relational, mentally-centred or physically-centred learners.

The first step in this circle involves the spirit and the ability to see. It begins with awareness in relation to self, family, community, nations and the universe.

The second step in the circle involves the heart and the ability to feel. This step requires the learner to make a decision to struggle personally with the new information and problems that arise. Some of the new information will contradict assumptions, beliefs and attitudes that the learner holds, causing an internal struggle.

---

11. Used with permission from Diane Hill, "Holistic Learning: A Model of Education Based on Aboriginal Cultural Philosophy" (unpublished master's thesis, St. Francis Xavier University, Antigonish, Nova Scotia, 1999). © Diane Hill, Ph.D. (abd). 1999. Unpublished Master's Thesis. Email: dianhill@worldchat.com

The third step in the circle involves the mind and the ability to know. The learner must resolve the contradictions encountered in the previous step and use these resolutions to build new knowledge.

The final step in the circle involves the body and the ability to do. This step represents preservation. Once the learner has experienced the awareness, struggle and building of the first three steps, a new sense of self can now be preserved.

Although the typical path through the circle of learning seems to begin with awareness and move toward action, it is possible for learners to move through the steps in any order; they may, for example, begin with their learning preference.

Teachers can consider this learning circle as they plan learning activities that will accommodate, engage and motivate students.

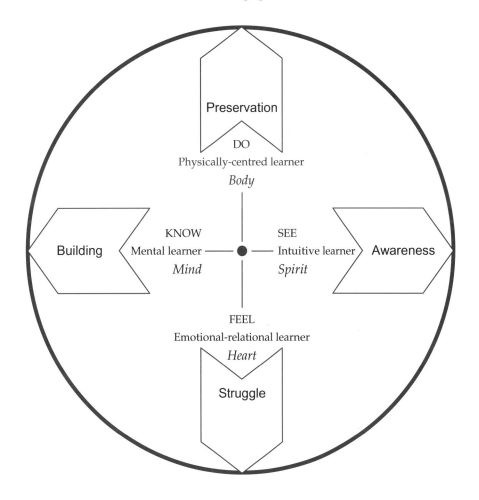

OUR WORDS, OUR WAYS

Shared wisdom

Using the circle to build understanding

"I have found that when I demonstrate with the circle and explain the never-ending spiral of awareness, struggle, building and preservation that an Aboriginal literacy learner experiences, the learners understand better their own learning capabilities. Sharing this information with them also helps to build their trust in me as a supportive and understanding practitioner."

– Swanson 2003, p. 64

Chapter 3

The Classroom:
A community of learners

This chapter will help teachers to:

- understand the impact of the classroom's physical environment on learning and take steps to create a safe, welcoming, engaging and respectful atmosphere
- understand the connections between the emotional environment and self-concept and learning success, and take steps to create a strong sense of community among students
- infuse Aboriginal content into the curriculum.

Many of the sample strategies and considerations have potential to benefit all students, not only Aboriginal students.

The classroom is more than simply a place. It is an environment that teachers and students create. When the atmosphere is warm, inclusive and inviting, students are more likely to feel safe and comfortable.

When they enter the classroom and sense a foundation of recognition and respect—cultural continuity—Aboriginal students feel better able to participate in classroom learning activities, take more ownership for their own learning, and face and overcome challenges that may lie ahead.

Shared wisdom

> **Living as a community**
> "The first stage of creating a learning community is to develop a sense of acceptance within the classroom. Learning to survive through tough winters has taught us [Aboriginal peoples] wonderful ways of living as a community. We have stories, laughter, quiet times of caring and all of the cooperative hard work that helps a community to survive … Living as a community in this way is absolutely essential to our youth."
>
> – Aboriginal teacher

Recent research into brain-based learning identifies the significance of the learner's affective or emotional state during the learning process. When students feel safe and comfortable, they are better able to learn.

Many Aboriginal students experience incidents of racism in school. They often say they do not feel safe in their schools or their classrooms.

Other Aboriginal students report that while students and teachers make an effort to welcome them into the school, they still often feel uncomfortable and like they do not belong.

A community of learners, where each student is recognized by his or her classmates and teachers as a valued and contributing member, can enhance a positive social-emotional environment that fosters success.

Living Systems

Aboriginal tradition views the community, and thus the education system, as a living process. Cree language, for example, distinguishes between animate and inanimate things differently than English. Many objects, such as tables and chairs, that would typically be considered nonliving in English, are often referred to as living objects in Cree.

Like any living thing, a living educational system needs to:
- breathe, to nourish itself
- be interdependent
- be sensitive to its environment and constantly receive feedback
- value the gifts that each different aspect brings to the whole.

The classroom must become a dynamic, living space that re-creates itself continually. This re-creation should be built on relationship, undertaken in dialogue with students and parents, and based on students' evolving learning needs.

Physical Environment

Traditionally, Aboriginal learning was often a multisensory small-group activity, beginning with observation and evolving into tactile, hands-on experiences. The classroom was the home and the village and, most significantly, the natural environment.

Shared wisdom

Traditional Aboriginal education
"Tribal teaching and learning were intertwined with the daily lives of both teacher and learner. Tribal education was a natural outcome of living in close communion with each other and the natural environment."

– Cajete 1994, p. 33

Consider how the physical arrangement of the classroom can affect the comfort level of students. The physical set-up of the classroom should offer the flexibility to incorporate many modes of learning. Adapting physical space by moving furniture and changing visual supports can be of benefit to all students. Ask students for their design ideas for the classroom environment. Brainstorm together for creative ideas and solutions.

Forming the Circle

The circle is a familiar and sacred shape in many Aboriginal cultures. From round dance to sharing circle, it symbolizes many things, including wholeness, inclusiveness and the cycles of life.

As a way to organize classroom seating, the circle is a form that encourages relationship, discussion and cooperation. Whether tables and desks are arranged in one large circle or several smaller circles, the arrangement helps to create a sense of community and cooperation within each circle—every student in the circle is equal. Some students prefer to work at round tables, or in desks clustered to make a working group.

Circular groupings encourage teachers to circulate throughout the room, making contact with individual learners.

story

Teacher

One big circle
"I've tried a lot of different desk and table arrangements over the years but the one that seems to work the best is one big circle. My own desk is part of the circle, too. When we all sit in a circle, we see each other's faces, we interact. The students seem more likely to take part, to become engaged with what we're doing. The centre of the circle becomes a space for all of us to use—for presentations, movement, games, drama—and for me to teach from. It makes it easy to move around and interact with each child."

Sounds, Sights and Movements

Aboriginal approaches to education see the classroom as a living system. A living system experiences changing levels of sound, light and sight, as well as movement.

43

Aboriginal students have preferences and needs relating to the level of intensity and input in each of these areas—and these may change from hour to hour and day to day. Consider the elements of sound, vision and movement, and experiment with them when creating the classroom atmosphere.

Sounds

Productive classroom work can range in volume from virtual silence to the noisy buzz of small-group project work. Consider the following sample strategies for ensuring the sounds of the classroom enhance student success.

- Vary activities so that the level and type of sound in the classroom varies.

- Provide alternate workspaces in quiet areas for students who are sensitive to aural distractions. Consider whether using a CD player and headset to listen to music as they work will be helpful.

- Use background music to create atmosphere.

- Encourage students to experiment with earplugs or headphones to see if this helps screen out distracting sounds.

- Consider using sound systems that amplify and clarify verbal interactions.

- Provide a quiet, distraction-free area for testing.

Sights

One significant way to create cultural continuity in the classroom is to routinely reflect Aboriginal experiences as part of visual displays and art projects. Ask contacts in the Aboriginal community (e.g., parents, Friendship Centres, Native liaison workers) to help collect posters, pictures, books and art for display in the classroom.

Consider using visual references for schedules and for steps in a sequence. These could be in the form of a planning board, list of activities or series of labelled pictures.

Fluorescent lights may have a negative impact on the concentration and learning of some students. By the end of the day, their eyes may be tired or they may get a headache. Whenever possible, use natural light or turn off some fluorescents during certain activities.

Movements

Students who learn well in a tactile, kinesthetic way benefit from active approaches to learning, such as building, modelling and demonstrating understanding through movement and drama. Providing these types of concrete experiences helps with both retention and comprehension of new skills and concepts.

Being able to move around freely may be especially important for some students. Creating opportunities for them to move around during learning activities can be a supportive step.

- Offer students the choice of standing, rather than sitting, for some activities.

- Plan times and activities that incorporate movement.

- Build in opportunities for movement during testing.

Emotional Environment: Culture and Self-concept

Aboriginal students are more likely to develop a positive self-concept in a classroom where their cultures are valued and their individual gifts are recognized. A strong self-concept is where learning and community both begin. It allows students to say "yes" to learning and to take their place in the classroom—"Yes, I can try this. Yes, I can do this. Yes, I will take part. Yes, I belong here. Yes, I am worth it."

A strong self-concept allows students to leave one classroom and go on to the next classroom or school with the ability to advocate for themselves and their learning needs.

As in all else, culture is at the core of a positive self-concept. Aboriginal students need to see positive reflections of their culture in the classroom on a regular basis, connected in meaningful ways to learning in all subject areas, at all grade levels, from science and math to literature and music.

Shared **wisdom**

Structure of doubt
"As the process of educational reform continues, it is imperative that researchers understand the structure of doubt the Canadian educational system has generated among Aboriginal people … The self-doubt it has generated within Aboriginal students has made them discount their inherent capacities and gifts."

– Battiste 2002, p. 27

45

Nurturing self-concept

Students enter the classroom on the first day of school with a self-concept that has already been influenced by past experiences beyond a teacher's control. But self-concepts can and do change—for better and for worse.

Traditionally, the community shared in the teaching of a young person. Students would be encouraged to discover their gifts and everyone involved understood that learning takes time. Many Aboriginal people are concerned that too few young people today understand the gift of being who they are. Without this understanding, students often feel lost and discouraged.

It is important for students to have a solid sense of who they are and of how their abilities allow them to contribute to the world around them. This sense of sustainability must come from deep within the student.

Teachers of Aboriginal students have an important role to play in nurturing the self-concepts of their students by:
- showing respect for and interest in Aboriginal cultures
- building cultural continuity into classroom activity
- creating a classroom environment that supports feelings of acceptance and respect
- expecting and finding ways to help every student succeed
- focusing on gifts and strengths, and encouraging students to use these to overcome their challenges
- helping students to recognize and own their successes—even the small ones
- communicating with parents and families about students' successes
- letting students make real decisions about things that will affect them, and expecting them to share responsibility for these decisions
- reminding students that they have the ability to make meaningful changes in the classroom, school and community, and providing them with opportunities to do so
- planning opportunities for students to contribute and feel connected by helping each other and the teacher
- helping students become effective self-advocates.

wisdom

Shared

> **Self-confidence**
> Developing a strong self-concept is not always easy—for sometimes life is hard. However, it is during some of our most difficult times that we can learn about some of the greatest gifts inside us. It is important for you to let your students know that gifts and wisdom are often earned by facing challenges wisely. Help them face the little things so they can grow strong in their gifts. As Hap Gilliland says, "… self-confidence is the memory of success" (1999, p. 79).

A sense of belonging

In Aboriginal traditions, cooperation and sharing are the foundations upon which families and communities base their survival. Competition and the accumulation of personal wealth often have significantly less status within Aboriginal communities than they do in mainstream society.

Aboriginal students are more likely to do their best work in classroom communities where they experience a sense of safety and belonging, and feel respected and valued as individuals within the group.

When teachers quietly and respectfully acknowledge the unique strengths of each individual student, students know they have an important place in the classroom. For many Aboriginal students, bragging and boasting are not considered culturally appropriate so it is important for the teacher to find ways to acknowledge students, without focusing unwelcome attention on them.

When students are able to identify their unique contributions to the classroom community, they also become aware of how to use their strengths and gifts to benefit the class as a whole. This process takes time and hard work, as well as an ongoing emphasis on equality among classroom members.

Uncovering hidden gifts

Helper, humourist, peacemaker, performer, artist, mathematician, observer—each student has a number of gifts they bring to the classroom.

To begin discovering students' classroom gifts, quietly observe them in group situations and one-on-one interactions with other students.

- How are students demonstrating their gifts? Do they hide or mask a strength? Do they misuse a strength?

- How can students' gifts enhance their learning?

If the students' gifts enhance their learning and growth, teachers can foster that strength by finding ways to acknowledge and use these gifts in classroom activities.

If gifts are misused in inappropriate behaviour, a student's gifts and strengths may be overlooked. For example, language and logic skills may be overlooked or dismissed in a student who likes to argue. Likewise, a student labelled as a troublemaker may have unrecognized leadership skills. The challenge is to help students recognize their own skills and then to encourage them to rechannel the skills in positive directions.

Modelling and reinforcing

A teacher's response to and respect for Aboriginal students, their cultures and their gifts will set the tone for other students. There are many opportunities to model respect, caring and acceptance.

- Ensure students are addressed by their correct names. Because of the effect of translation, some students' surnames may sound unusual. If they have a surname such as "Calf Robe," do not abbreviate it, for example, to "Calf"—use their full name.

- Remember and refer to students' personal interests so that they feel important and accepted.

- Do not allow put-downs of anyone. Teach students strategies for responding to put-downs, such as being assertive and saying, "That is a put-down and I will not accept it."

- Find ways to recognize students' strengths on a regular basis, in both one-on-one settings and group settings. Many Aboriginal peoples do not promote the praise of individuals. Recognize or celebrate strengths in the context of the contribution students have made to the community—to another student's success, to a team effort or to the class as a whole.

- Widen appreciation and acceptance by planning activities that highlight Aboriginal cultures as well as the strengths, talents and interests of individual students.

- Teach, model and reinforce social skills.

story

Teacher

Classroom rules
"I tell my students that rules and guidelines exist so we can all use our gifts wisely and contribute to our community.

When we create our classroom rules, I contribute 50 percent of the rules and the students develop the other 50 percent. We read the rules aloud and practise them every day. I try especially hard to live by the rules. Because the students have input into the rules, they really mean a lot to them—they want their classroom to function well.

I also try to acknowledge and reinforce students who use their gifts and make a contribution."

Using peer mentors and tutors

Look for opportunities for Aboriginal students, particularly those who struggle with their academic or social skills, to be peer tutors for other students. Have them tutor in an area of strength or about a concept they have already mastered. Not only will this boost their self-concept, it will help clarify and reinforce what they have learned. Teaching is often the best way to learn.

Peer mentors can help students develop social and friendship skills. Peer mentors can serve as role models, sources of information, readers, scribes and study buddies. Because they speak the same "language" and often have similar experiences, peer mentors can help create a more relaxed learning situation. Be aware that the best students are often not the best tutors; they may not be able to relate to the learning challenges and struggles that other students face.

Peer tutoring can benefit Aboriginal students, both when they tutor and when they are the ones being tutored.

story

Teacher

Sharing gifts
"One boy in my Grade 6 class is just an amazing artist. He struggles with language skills but he communicates beautifully through his art. The Grade 8 teacher was doing an art unit in an area where his gift really shines and she suggested that he come into her class and basically teach this lesson. He got such a lift from that experience! It was so good for him."

49

Encouraging leadership

In Aboriginal traditions, leadership is taught through service—helping others is a critical component of learning. Traditionally, being a good helper is an important value to live by. If people help one another with kindness, things will go well. Silent leadership, or living in "right relationship" with others, can be a very powerful learning force. Aboriginal students need opportunities to create change in their classrooms, their schools and in our complex world.

To encourage student leadership, teachers can use strategies such as the following.

- Develop leadership among students by looking for opportunities to have them help other students as well as teachers.

- Help students understand that they are often in a position to help, for example, they can plan an event or help a classmate with homework.

- Assure students (and their parents) that they have the right and responsibility to ask questions of teachers, and to discuss issues that they may have differing views on. Some students and their families have limited experience questioning others. To be good leaders, they need to learn to do this with confidence, respect and a willingness to consider multiple perspectives.

story

Teacher

"At our school, all the students from grades 4 through 9 do Group Fit and Group Cree together. We use a family model that's familiar to the students, where the older kids help with the younger ones. The students like it and it lets the older ones take a leadership role. We also find that for the older students to teach the younger ones, they really need to know their stuff."

Building community through talking circles

Talking circles are based on the sacred tradition of sharing circles. People leading a traditional sharing circle have a blessing from an Elder to do this, and use special prayers and sacred objects in the ceremony. Consider inviting an Elder to the classroom to help students learn about this tradition.

The purpose of the less formal talking circle, used as part of classroom instruction, is to create a safe environment where students can share their point of view with others. Create a talking circle in the classroom, where all the students come together to solve problems, explore issues or celebrate successes. Circles are useful when the topic under consideration has no right or wrong answer, or when classroom members need to share their feelings or thoughts.

Within the circle, each member has equality—no one is above or below anyone else. What each member says will be listened to without interruption and without criticism. Talking circles ensure that everyone has a chance to speak, so even quiet students have the opportunity to participate and be heard. It also creates opportunities for participants to develop an empathetic appreciation for points of view other than their own.

It takes the contributions of each member within the circle to make the classroom community work well. Creating opportunities for students to have real input into real decisions about what happens in the classroom is an effective way of teaching about:

- *consequences*—seeing their ideas put into action; learning about the direct results of choices and decisions
- *respect*—hearing other students' needs and opinions; having their own needs and opinions heard
- *responsibility*—to themselves, each other and the teacher
- *trust*—trusting themselves and each other to make good decisions; living up to the teacher's trust in them to make good decisions
- *leadership*—putting ideas into action; working toward the common good; thinking for themselves
- *community*—valuing everyone; balancing the needs of individuals with the needs of the group.

If a topic is a very sensitive one, a teacher may wish to invite an Elder to provide leadership. With sensitive topics there is always the risk of students making themselves vulnerable through sharing or receiving information. Sensitive topics may evoke an array of emotions. This can result in things that should not be getting said, or sensitive and inappropriate personal information being shared. Teachers need to ensure that no individual student is left vulnerable or hurt by what is said in the talking circle. Teachers must also be prepared to provide support for students who share information that reveals a specific need or risk.

For a blackline master on guidelines for talking circles, see *Appendix 5: Guidelines for Talking Circles.*

wisdom

Shared

> **Symbolism of the circle**
> "In Native tradition, the Circle is a symbol of power, relation, peace and unity. It serves as a reminder of the sacred relationship we share with all living beings in this world and of our responsibility as a helper and contributor to the flow of the Circle of Life by living in harmony and balance with all our relations."
>
> – Garrett et al. 2003, p. 227

Aboriginal Content

While the first responsibility for teachers is to follow the provincial programs of study, the content and context used to teach these outcomes can be a powerful message to students. To Aboriginal students especially, Aboriginal content—whether in a story, a math example or a problem-solving technique—can have a profound impact on how they see themselves. It can also affect their understanding of how others see them and their cultures.

A *lack* of Aboriginal content in the classroom also speaks volumes. Without opportunities to reflect on their histories and cultures—and to engage with their peers in this reflection—Aboriginal students may feel isolated, unheard and invisible.

Unfortunately there are many images—both visual and written—created by individuals with limited understanding of Aboriginal peoples and cultures. Most of these images have been, and continue to be, harmful, damaging the self-concept of Aboriginal people and teaching non-Aboriginal people false concepts. It is important that individual teachers be vigilant to ensure that these inaccurate and hurtful images do not find their way into the classroom.

Fortunately, there is an increasing range of positive Aboriginal content available in many media and across many subject areas, from literature and visual art to film, music, science, mathematics, and so on.

The First Nations, Métis and Inuit (FNMI) Curriculum Infusion Project is part of the Alberta Education First Nations, Métis and Inuit Initiative. The objective is to increase the relevance of provincial programs of study for all students by:
- infusing Aboriginal perspectives into programs of study
- providing strategies for implementation of these programs of study that will support and encourage all students, including Aboriginal students.

Aboriginal content can happen in two ways: as specific programs of study on Aboriginal content and as infusion of Aboriginal content into existing programs of study.

Specific Aboriginal content

These programs of study are specifically designed to focus on Aboriginal peoples, cultures, worldviews and contemporary issues. This includes selected focus on Aboriginal peoples in the new Kindergarten to Grade 12 Social Studies program, in the senior high Aboriginal Studies 10, 20, 30 program, and in the new nine-year and twelve-year Cree and Blackfoot Language and Culture programs currently under development.

Infusion of Aboriginal content

Aboriginal content can be infused into the regular Kindergarten to Grade 12 programs of study. Infusion of Aboriginal content is not an add-on or a special event—it is an integral, embedded and ongoing aspect of classroom experience. This inclusive model includes infusion of Aboriginal perspectives across the subject areas at all grade levels.

The infusion of Aboriginal content into the regular curriculum ensures that all students have opportunities to learn about the historical and contemporary contributions and cultures of Aboriginal peoples.

In a classroom that includes Aboriginal students, infusion of Aboriginal content provides a balance of perspectives and helps dispel stereotypes by reflecting these students' cultures in their learning. Students learn most effectively when they experience a connection with what they are learning. Infusion fosters this connection. It also encourages Aboriginal students to become aware of the multiple perspectives within Aboriginal groups.

In a classroom of both Aboriginal and non-Aboriginal students, infusion of Aboriginal content encourages all students to become more aware of their own perspectives on particular topics or concepts, and to increase their knowledge and understanding of Aboriginal perspectives.

Infusion of Aboriginal content also offers students a way to study the universal human experience within the Aboriginal experience. Just as students learn about human dynamics from Shakespeare or a Margaret Laurence novel, so too can students identify with the life dynamics presented by characters and situations in an Aboriginal film such as *Smoke Signals* or by an Aboriginal novelist such as Thomas King.

Cultural infusion is:
- congruent with the Alberta programs of study
- comfortable with complexity, with "this AND that"
- an attitude, an awareness
- a permeation, rather than an add-on or drop-in piece of information.

Cultural Infusion and the Non-Aboriginal Teacher

How does a non-Aboriginal teacher ensure that infusion of Aboriginal content is appropriate, follows protocol and maintains cultural integrity? The key is to rely on Aboriginal resources including:
- print, video and film, visual art, and other resources created by Aboriginal people
- contacts in the Aboriginal community made through cultural liaisons, parents and community leaders, keeping in mind that different people hold varying levels and diverse areas of expertise.

Selecting Aboriginal Content

When choosing a work, such as a piece of literature or art, or an activity to infuse into the regular curriculum, give careful consideration to:
- voice and source
- intent
- complexity.

Voice and source

The effectiveness of any work—such as a short story, a historical text or a contemporary film—as an infusion of content depends to a large extent on the voice or tone it embodies and on its source or authorship.

To assess the appropriateness of a work's voice, ask questions such as the following.

- Is the material respectful and truthful in both tone and information?

- Is there anything in the material that could embarrass or hurt an Aboriginal or non-Aboriginal student?

- Could the material foster stereotypical thinking in either Aboriginal or non-Aboriginal students?

- Does the material present a one-sided view of history, religion or lifestyles? Does it measure success in life by only one standard?

- Does the material present Aboriginal cultures and peoples as distinct from one another, or does it portray pan-Indianism (a generic presentation of "Indian" culture)?

- Does the work reflect respect for the roles of women and Elders in Aboriginal cultures?

- Is the language respectful and free of any racist or insulting words or images?

- Do Aboriginal characters speak dialogue that reflects the language skills of oral traditions, or do they speak Hollywood-style—simplistic language or "noble savage" dialogue?

To assess the appropriateness of a work's source or authorship, ask questions such as the following.

- What is the author's (or artist's or filmmaker's) background or experience that qualifies him or her to portray Aboriginal peoples and cultures?

- Does the author's perspective strengthen or enhance the portrayal of Aboriginal peoples, cultures or issues?

Intent

To assess the intent of a work, ask questions such as the following.

- Does the work interpret ways of life with a deep knowledge of them? Non-Aboriginals are seldom intimately familiar with or deeply knowledgeable about the realities of Aboriginal contemporary and traditional ways of life.

- Does the work present a balanced, factual view? Or does it describe events in terms that state or imply the superiority of one group over another?

- Does the work attribute advances to one group but not another? For example, does it name the European explorer but not the Aboriginal people who guided the explorer to "his" discoveries?

For a blackline master of a sample checklist, see *Appendix 6: Evaluating Resources About Aboriginal Peoples.*

Complexity

When choosing an activity, make sure that it is presented and undertaken in a way that reflects, as closely as possible, the daily, lived experience of that activity. Separating an activity from its social or spiritual context removes its underlying significance and cultural integrity. Consider the following examples.

- Bannock making connects to teaching about sharing. When students are making bannock, invite another class to share it with them. (Serve it with black tea, butter and jam.)

- Making miniature tipis is in itself simply a craft activity, not a cultural learning experience. When an Elder or traditional teacher guides the students through the teachings associated with each tipi pole and the symbols painted on the tipi, tipi making becomes cultural infusion.

Process for infusing Aboriginal content

The effective infusion of Aboriginal content goes hand in hand with a learning process that reflects the tenets of Aboriginal education. This is a time-generous, rather than time-limited, approach that is cooperative rather than competitive. It also incorporates a holistic approach, encourages observation, is experiential, is based in community resources and considers multiple perspectives.

Holistic approach

Successful infusion encourages curriculum crossovers, such as telling Aboriginal legends as part of science, discussing Aboriginal literature in language arts, learning Aboriginal activities and games in physical education or using the geometric ratios of the traditional star quilt to teach mathematics.

Observation

Students learn from modelling and demonstration. For example, they watch as a tipi is erected, then try it themselves.

Experiential

Students learn in hands-on ways, by doing. For example, students could create art and text styled on the works of Aboriginal artist George Littlechild to explore and express family and community relationships.

Based in the community's resources

Elders, parents, liaisons and community leaders bring a variety of traditions—oral, written, visual—into the teachings. For example, an Aboriginal lawyer could talk to a social studies class about his or her work in restorative justice.

Considers multiple perspectives

The process of infusing Aboriginal content does not seek to polarize views; it reflects a "this AND that" point of view. For example, the history of residential schools reflects many viewpoints.

Assessment

With infusion of Aboriginal content, effective and appropriate assessment and evaluation should evolve out of the process so that what is being measured is a growth of awareness and a change in attitude. To be truly meaningful, evaluation needs to address more than mastery of specific skills or information.

The objective of cultural infusion is an increased understanding of and appreciation for multiple perspectives. Self-reflection becomes an important component in assessing how infused content affects learning, because it is through self-reflection that hearts and minds are opened.

Assessment processes can be both subjective and objective, and both structured and unstructured. For more structured types of assessment, rubrics can be used to clarify tasks and expectations.

Wherever possible, the assessment should reflect the cultural perspective being presented. For example, in an activity on consensus decision making, the most appropriate type of assessment would be a performance task that demonstrates how students actually participate in decision making.

Use of Literature

Literature—especially works by Aboriginal authors—encourages Aboriginal students to increase their knowledge and understanding of the world and of themselves. It allows them to identify with the experiences of characters in situations both familiar and new, and in the case of Aboriginal literature, to experience cultural continuity in their classrooms.

The literary genre of storytelling is especially valued by Aboriginal cultures; teaching through literature is a core tenet of Aboriginal approaches to education. Aboriginal students may already be very familiar with the use of storytelling as a teaching tool, both at home and in the classroom.

Use literature to encourage students to:
- examine ways they connect with the story and the characters
- explore their own ideas and beliefs
- develop problem-solving skills
- incorporate hopeful strategies to draw upon in the future.

Literature can also foster cross-curricular connections. Look for authentic ways to link outcomes in science, social studies, health and other subjects with themes in novels, stories, films and poems.

Students can respond to literature at any stage of reading by:
- making predictions prior to reading a story
- stopping at various points in the story to make a comment, respond to what is happening or make further predictions
- responding to what they read through a variety of activities.

There are many ways to respond to a work of literature, including:
- journal writing
- letters to a character
- drawings (for example, drawing pictures of various options a character might have or of personal experiences evoked by the story)
- role-plays based on a story
- revisions to the story, including writing different endings or sequels to the story.

The new authorized list of grades 4–12 novels includes a number of works by contemporary Aboriginal writers. A list of these novels is posted on the Alberta Education Web site at www.education.gov.ab.ca/k_12/curriculum/bySubject/english/novel 4_12.pdf.

Consider whether or not the school library might contain outdated material that promotes misinformation and stereotyping. If so, do a systematic culling of inappropriate materials so that students are accessing reliable and culturally appropriate information when they use the school library.

Selecting Aboriginal Images

Consider the following guidelines when selecting pictures, photographs and other Aboriginal images to use in the classroom.

Keep the images human
Often, images of Aboriginal people can objectify them—they become objects to count, animal caricatures or team mascots.

Represent the diversity of Aboriginal peoples
There are over 500 First Nations groups in North America, in addition to the Métis and Inuit peoples. Avoid pan-Indianistic viewpoints that portray all Aboriginal peoples as coming from the plains area. Not all First Nations people were buffalo hunters or tipi dwellers.

Recognize the complexity of Aboriginal societies

Aboriginal communities have always consisted of a variety of specialized, skilled roles for both men and women including hunters, entertainers, healers and teachers. Images should reflect the diversity and complexity of these communities. Avoid images that reflect only a limited perspective of the community—such as men only as warriors, or women only as caregivers.

Include contemporary as well as historical images

It is important to choose images that show Aboriginal people in contemporary as well as historical times. Contemporary images reflect the evolving and adaptable nature of Aboriginal communities. Examples of these images may include housing in the North (not just igloos), national Aboriginal councils involved in political decision making, or traditional dancers using new materials and colours for their regalia. It is important for images to reflect the reality that Aboriginal people still exist in today's society.

Chapter 4

School, Family and Community:
Sharing the responsibility

This chapter will help teachers to:
- appreciate the value for all students of positive school involvement with Aboriginal family and community members
- understand the significance of creating school and classroom environments that welcome Aboriginal parents
- understand the role of the school/community liaison worker
- understand and follow protocols for communicating with, welcoming and showing appreciation for Elders and other Aboriginal guests to the classroom
- understand and follow protocols for arranging a visit to an Aboriginal community.

In traditional Aboriginal life, mothers and fathers, grandmothers and grandfathers, aunts and uncles, brothers and sisters, Elders and the greater community shared the responsibility for educating the children. Young people saw the skills and knowledge they were developing embodied among the people in their families and community. Today, with increased mobility and disruption of families, this traditional means of education is breaking down.

When schools and teachers make an effort to invite Aboriginal families and community members to take part in classroom and schoolwide activities, Aboriginal children have a valuable opportunity to interact with role models who reflect their cultures. Their non-Aboriginal classmates also benefit from relating to and learning from adults with worldviews different than their own. Aboriginal visitors are especially important role models in the school community because there are currently so few Aboriginal teachers.

Research shows that parental involvement results in higher student achievement and safer school environments. Studies also show that for students who are at-risk, parent and family involvement is the single most important determinant of success (Mills 1994 cited in Kavanagh n.d.).

61

The vision of success for Aboriginal children includes classrooms and schools where:

- Aboriginal families and community members feel welcome and comfortable
- the physical environment reflects a respect for Aboriginal cultures
- Aboriginal parents and community members participate to create responsive and rich programming
- there are frequent opportunities for positive interaction among Aboriginal and non-Aboriginal people of all ages.

Teachers can help make this vision a reality in the classroom and the school by creating a welcoming environment for parents, Elders and other Aboriginal guests. Aboriginal parents, families and community members will begin to feel welcome in a school environment that expresses knowledge of and respect for Aboriginal cultures, and values their involvement.

Parents and community members will feel more welcome when the physical and visual elements of the school and classroom reflect an informal, comfortable atmosphere that celebrates diversity. This could include:

- art by students and others, such as posters, wall hangings, displays of books and CDs that reflect Aboriginal peoples and their cultures
- a room or a space for Elders to use as needed
- setting aside a space with a change table, picture books and appropriate toys for parents with young children
- tea, coffee, water and bannock or other snacks.

Ask parents for their ideas about how to create a welcoming environment.

Welcoming Parents

Like all parents, Aboriginal parents play a vital part in the success of their children. (The term parent also refers to significant others including extended families and guardian relationships.)

A key to welcoming Aboriginal parents is to establish a positive relationship with them as soon as their children join the class. This will help ensure that a teacher is not contacting parents for the first time if and when a problem arises. Invite parents to:

- meet informally in the classroom or, if this is not practical, ask to visit them in their home or at a friendship centre, recreation centre or Métis/band office
- attend student presentations, portfolio reviews and other activities throughout the school year.

Ask parents for their insight and suggestions on how to build cultural continuity in the classroom and the school. Invite them to:

- contribute their knowledge about their cultures to curriculum-related activities
- contribute their talents to classroom and schoolwide activities such as organizational skills or carpentry, craft and creative skills.

story

Liaison

Parent involvement

"Once we started asking our Aboriginal parents to take an active part in what we're doing, we found so many ways to involve them! We have parents teaching conversational Cree, grandparents teaching about traditional values, parents inviting artists from the community to visit our school, parents who are dancers and musicians themselves."

Time and place

Being flexible about when, how and where you involve parents and families creates more opportunities to connect with them. Many Aboriginal parents are working and busy with family and community commitments. They may find it difficult to participate in activities or attend meetings during school hours. Increase parent involvement with the school by considering the following strategies.

- When scheduling classroom and school events, consider the work hours of your parents and how to best accommodate them.

- Arrange for childcare during family events at the school.

- Offer to meet with parents at their home.

- Offer parents who are unable to volunteer during school hours other options for contributing.

- Be sensitive to the fact that some families may be dealing with economic stress. Consider this when setting field-trip fees, asking for contributions for bake sales or planning events that involve transportation.

story

Liaison

Parent volunteer

"My colleagues were originally very reluctant to support a parent coming into our school to teach cultural activities. They were concerned about confidentiality—worried that she might overhear something in the staff room about other students and families. They were also concerned about her younger child coming to school with her. I was sure this mom would be a really strong support for our students so I worked very hard to convince my colleagues to give her a chance—I spoke with the mom about confidentiality and we set up a play space for her kids in the classroom. In the end, it worked out very well. Both the teachers and students loved her!"

Meaningful involvement

Above all, Aboriginal parents seek meaningful involvement with their child's program and learning team. In her review of First Nations parent and community involvement in schools, Barbara Kavanagh (n.d.) makes the following suggestions for meaningful parent involvement.

- Recognize that parents have a genuine right to be involved in decision making and activities. Successful parent involvement is student-centred and ongoing.

- Help parents understand their rights, and the procedures and protocols to follow if they disagree with school decisions. All school authorities are required to have a process in place for parents to appeal decisions at the local level. Each reserve school has its own policy in place—and policies may differ from one federally run school to the next.

- Develop strategies with parents, not for parents. Invite parents to actively participate in decisions concerning their child. Schedule meetings around their availability. Ensure that they are kept up-to-date through classroom newsletters or phone calls.

- Do not underestimate parents and families. Set high standards for their involvement. Recognize parents' strengths and commend them for the ways they support their children's education and learning. If problems with involvement come up, try to look at the situation from the parents' point of view. Recognize when differences in worldviews and issues such as economic and other stresses create barriers to involvement. Be flexible.

- Be clear about the importance of regular attendance at school. Help parents and students understand the benefits and work collaboratively to develop strategies that support and enhance student attendance.

- Help parents find support and programs in the community.

- Recognize that meaningful parent involvement will take many forms. Parents have differing personal histories related to school experiences, comfort levels, interests and strengths. Look for ways to value and use every parent's unique insights and talents. Ask parents how they would like to be involved. Encourage them to increase their involvement at a pace that is comfortable for them.

- Consider how student-led conferences could enhance parent involvement. Help students develop formats and practise the skills needed to effectively and meaningfully share their learning with their families.

Effective communication

When communicating with parents about their child's learning progress and challenges:
- balance positive comments with comments about concerns
- describe students' behaviours in nonjudgemental language. For example, "Alex often needs to have instructions repeated several times"
- avoid blaming.

Do not mistake a nondirective approach for a lack of concern. Parents who live by the principle of noninterference may feel that it is appropriate for them not to become involved, since teachers are the professionals. Use information from research and classroom examples to show parents how their involvement will benefit their children.

story

Teacher

The classroom as a meeting place

One teacher shared her experience with parent involvement in a class of secondary students:

"In an indigenous family, parents, aunts, uncles, grandparents and all forms of an extended family are significant in the lives of the students and therefore, the school. One of the reasons why I use monthly presentations of learning is for the extended families to feel welcome in the school and to also begin to increase the understanding of provincial curriculums within the community. In urban, multicultural classrooms, it is important for a school to be a centre of community, bridging many cultures. I planned monthly presentations by each student to their parents and others. On the first parent evening, I had each student guide their parents to their work area. They reviewed the curriculum for their grade. Then they presented their work

(continued)

story

Teacher

The classroom as a meeting place (continued)
and showed a video of their in-class presentations. The videos gave the students and their families a chance to see the classroom process and allowed the students to reflect back on their presentation skills. The parents completed a feedback form of their perceptions of the student's strengths and the areas that they could work on. They were also invited to write any questions that they had and to offer suggestions for future nights.

The classroom became a meeting place. Parents visited with one another and shared in the work of other students. Clusters formed and families began to talk about their experiences.

Later that week, students asked me if their parents could come into the classroom during the day. Students who had previously said, "I don't want my parents near this place" were now changing their minds. I had parents phoning me and asking me more questions about how their son or daughter was learning. They wanted to know more about the curriculum so that they could help. They were involved. The previous year I had only five parents come to parent conferences. Now I have parents volunteering all over the place.

The neatest stuff, though, is in the more subtle changes. I've seen families come together that had been struggling. I've seen teens wanting their parents to be involved for the first time in years.

One family comes to mind. The grandparents of one girl invited our whole class to come and visit them at their lakeside home in the northern part of the province. The entire family—parents, grandparents and kids—were all involved. A year before, that young girl wanted to leave her home. This girl now has a personal mission—she wants to work in a developing country as a nurse. Her family is actively supporting her mission and her daily attendance in school. Last year she spent a large part of the year away from school. This year, so far she hasn't missed a day."

Resolving differences

If parents become frustrated, be careful not to minimize their concerns, argue or become defensive. In many Aboriginal cultures, those who display their tempers lose respect. Consider the following strategies.

- Let parents know that what they say is important.

- Write down the concerns or suggestions of parents.

- Ask parents to clarify if the concerns are too general.

- Work on solutions together. Write them down.

Parent advocacy

Advocacy means speaking out and taking positive action to make a situation better. For example, Aboriginal parents may want to advocate for extra help for their child in school, for building on their child's special interests or for culturally relevant approaches to instruction or to discipline. This can be a challenge for some Aboriginal parents who may not feel comfortable in a school environment.

Depending on their experience, some parents may be unsure of how to advocate on their children's behalf. Some parents also may be reluctant to do so because they may not want to interfere in what they see as the school's business. They may also want to avoid conflict or feel that they will not be listened to.

Parents need to know how advocacy will help their child. They need to see teachers modelling this process. If the school has an Aboriginal liaison, it might be appropriate to involve the liaison in the advocacy process.

To help parents become more effective advocates for their children, consider the following strategies.

- Before contacting other teachers, school staff and professionals on a student's behalf, consult with the student's parents and seek their advice and support.

- Include parents in preparations for meetings. Share information and ask for their input on agendas and who should be invited to meetings.

- Model appropriate language when talking to parents about their child's learning concerns. Model the collaborative "win-win" attitude of successful advocates.

- Involve parents in meetings with other teachers and consultants. Encourage them to observe the process of collaboration and problem solving with others.

- Commend parents for their efforts at advocacy.

- Share information with parents such as the following suggestions that Aboriginal parents share in the Alberta Education resource, *A Handbook for Aboriginal Parents of Children with Special Needs* (2000).

67

Shared

wisdom

Aboriginal parents offer advice to other parents

- Come to the school—the school belongs to your child. Visit your child's school anytime throughout the school year. At the beginning of the year, ask your child's teacher how to make arrangements to visit the classroom.

- Let your voice be heard by the teacher and, if need be, by the administration. If you have a concern, continue to speak up, as it is the only way positive changes will happen.

- Ask to sit in on classes to see what is happening.

- Talk with other parents who have children in the class.

- Look for local parent support groups and find out about other resources.

- Get to know the teacher by name and make sure he or she knows how to contact you.

- Tell the teacher how you may be contacted if you don't have a phone.

- Make an appointment with the teacher to discuss any specific concerns. Make arrangements to telephone or write a letter if you are unable to meet.

- Ask that the teacher, principal, liaison worker or school counsellor meet with you in your home if you would feel more comfortable meeting there.

- Read the school newsletters, as they often contain valuable information that concerns your child.

- Become familiar with the school's policies and procedures about attendance, discipline and other issues.

- Don't be afraid to ask questions.

- Go to all parent-teacher conferences.

- Keep all school information in one place so it's handy for meetings at the school or when seeing others in the community about your child.

- Volunteer to share a craft or special skill from your culture.

Adapted from Alberta Learning, *A Handbook for Aboriginal Parents of Children with Special Needs* (Edmonton, AB: Alberta Learning, 2000), pp. 30–31.

For a blackline master of these suggestions, see *Appendix 7: Aboriginal Parents Offer Advice to Other Parents*.

Liaison Workers

A number of school districts are finding that liaison workers, employed at either the district or school level, can be important sources of information and support for Aboriginal students and their families. Job descriptions for liaison workers across the province vary, but they often include the following types of responsibilities:

- establishing and maintaining a trusting relationship with Aboriginal students and their families
- acting as a communication link between home and school to assist with school-related issues
- meeting with individual students on a regular basis to find out what these students need
- connecting with Aboriginal organizations and community services so they can refer and connect students and families to the community resources they need
- providing assistance to teachers for presentations related to Aboriginal cultures, issues and languages
- organizing cultural events and activities for the school community.

In-depth knowledge of Aboriginal cultures, communities and languages is key to the success of liaison workers.

Liaison workers can help increase the involvement of Aboriginal families in their children's education and can reduce the effects of discrimination and racism for these students. The efforts of liaison workers can contribute to improved student attendance, achievement, self-confidence and decision making. Having a liaison worker in the school can also promote the development and implementation of appropriate cultural and educational services for Aboriginal students.

story

Principal

Role of the liaison worker
"I had a lot to learn as a new principal. Although as a teacher, I always enjoyed positive relationships with the families of my Aboriginal students, I was finding it more difficult to reach parents in my new role as administrator. In retrospect, I guess I really didn't understand how truly negative many of the families felt toward anything to do with school and education. A principal represents authority for some people, and for some Aboriginal parents, this can stir up many negative memories of their own personal experience with schooling. At the beginning of the school year, I was having difficulty getting parents to return my phone calls or meet with me.

(continued)

69

Principal story

Role of the liaison worker (continued)
Connie, the Aboriginal liaison worker at the school, really helped me build my knowledge base and learn the community protocol that first year. She also shared background information about families with me. This helped me develop a better understanding of not only the kinds of challenges these families faced but also the strengths and gifts these families had. She offered me, and other teachers on staff, practical ideas for making sure our Aboriginal families feel welcome at the school. She would often pave the way for us by meeting informally with a family before we phoned them or asked them to come for a meeting. With her guidance, the staff also began to do more home visits and use talking circles for meetings.

As a liaison worker, Connie had many roles in the school. In addition to coordinating cultural events, she organized a number of low-key opportunities for parents to come into the school, such as coffee mornings and beading classes. This really helped create a new comfort level for many of the parents. This informal socializing also gave her opportunities to talk one-on-one with parents, and by doing this, she found out what was going on in their lives and then was better able to offer support and advice.

The whole community valued the preventive work she did on behalf of our students. Using her excellent connections in the community, she was able to help a number of families put much-needed supports into place before problems escalated into full-blown crisis situations. The number of families in the school needing formal Child Welfare involvement dropped significantly after her first year on staff.

Connie also developed strong relationships with individual students. In our annual school survey, Aboriginal students consistently identified Connie's most important role as being 'someone at school who really understands and cares about me.'"

Welcoming Elders

Elders are men and women regarded as the keepers and teachers of an Aboriginal nation's oral tradition and knowledge. Age is not considered a determinant of wisdom; young people of sixteen years may have essential knowledge. Different Elders hold different gifts. Their contributions to schools and classrooms can be significant when they are involved in meaningful ways such as bringing traditional ceremonies and teachings into the school or classroom; providing advice to parents, students, teachers and school administrators; providing accurate information about Aboriginal heritage and Aboriginal communities; and acting as a bridge between the school and the community.

Elders are considered vital to the survival of Aboriginal cultures and the transmission of cultural knowledge is an essential part of the preservation and promotion of cultural traditions and their protocols. Elders are always to be treated with great respect and honour.

The roles of Elders vary greatly from community to community, as do the protocols and traditions they teach. Elders can be spiritual guides, healers, medicine men and women, artists, seers and counsellors. Elders often perform such services as:
- giving prayers before meetings
- describing or performing traditional ceremonies
- sharing traditional knowledge
- giving spiritual advice to individuals
- demonstrating traditional crafts and practices
- teaching the community's protocols.

The wisdom of Elders can be divided into two types: spiritual advice and traditional knowledge. According to Elders' teachings, spiritual advice is the teachings of prayers to the Creator for personal well-being or ceremonial activities. Traditional knowledge has to do with knowing how to live in a way that is respectful to Mother Earth.

It is important to make Elders welcome by following protocol or a code of etiquette appropriate to the customs of the people or community. *In Alberta, each Aboriginal community has its own cultural and social traditions that translate into protocols that should be carefully followed.* Although regional and tribe-specific protocols have evolved over time, there are many similarities and common themes that are important to remember.

Using proper protocol means following the customs of the people or community. As protocol varies between communities and individuals, it is important to ask an informed community member about the protocol that needs to be followed. Generally, people respect those who care enough to ask.

71

story

Principal

Elder in the school

"In the past, if there was a problem, we would set up a meeting with a counsellor or a community agency for our Aboriginal families and more often than not, the family would choose not to take that route with the problem. When we began working with an Elder, we saw a distinct change in the families' response—they would attend meetings where the Elder would be present, and often, the Elder's parenting circle as well. As an added benefit, students regularly seek out our Elder to talk about personal issues."

story

Liaison

Elders' support

"We had an escalating situation with one high school student. The school's administrators had reached their limit and called in the parents. Having heard their son's side of the story, the parents were extremely angry with the school. There didn't seem to be much of a chance of resolving anything, everyone was so upset. So we requested the help of two Elders, a man and a woman, to mediate at a meeting between the administrators, the student and the parents. They met in a conference room rather than the administrator's office. They sat in a talking circle, not across a desk from each other. Everyone's attitude began to shift when they heard the other person's side of the story. This process had a lasting effect—the student is still struggling with school but because he's stopped challenging authority, he's finding the support he needs."

Approaching an Elder

The best way to contact an Elder and learn the protocols to follow is to ask contacts in the community, such as Aboriginal liaisons in the school system, parents or Friendship Centre staff. Community members will be able to provide the names of respected Elders.

For a list of Aboriginal organizations and agencies that can advise schools on choosing and working with local Elders, see *Appendix 8: Aboriginal Organizations and Agencies*.

These community members can help teachers determine which Elders would be appropriate visitors to the school or classroom. For example, one Elder might have significant knowledge of a ceremony, while other Elders might be knowledgeable about the history of the community or a traditional skill.

Aboriginal people believe that if you want to know something, you must be willing to sit with someone who has the knowledge. Be aware that when you approach an Elder, you must be patient.

Other potential topics for Elder presentations include:
- kinship
- role modelling
- parenting
- importance of education
- planning for the future.

When approaching a First Nations or Métis Elder, protocol *usually* requires the offering of tobacco, a sacred traditional plant that is used to open the door to consult with Elders. An Aboriginal liaison or Elder's helper can provide the necessary guidance when determining when tobacco is necessary. Consider the following guidelines when offering tobacco to an Elder.

- When the Elder indicates that he or she is ready and introductions have been made, state your request in a respectful way. Be clear, open and honest, and speak plainly. For example,

  "We would be honoured if you would give a prayer at our next meeting."

  "I would be honoured to benefit from your advice and guidance."

  "We would be honoured if you would visit our class to share your knowledge on ..."

  It is also important for the Elder to understand what kind of guidance you are requesting: spiritual advice or traditional knowledge.

- If the Elder accepts the tobacco from you, he or she is accepting your invitation or request. The tobacco will then be offered to the Creator during a prayer for life and good health.

  If the Elder declines the tobacco, he or she is declining your invitation or request. The Elder may have prior commitments or be unable to help you. Ask your community contact for clarification.

Hosting Elders in the classroom

Elders are respected community members and should be treated well. Elders are very humble and do not ask for anything, but they are usually busy people, and the gift of time and wisdom they bring needs to be valued. Consider the following guidelines for hosting an Elder in the classroom.

- Ensure that transportation, accommodation and meals are taken care of, either by providing them or by giving an honorarium to cover expenses. Sometimes an Elder may need to be driven to an event. If an Elder brings a helper, their costs should be covered, as well.

- Prepare the students for the visit from the Elder by reviewing good listening practices and manners such as avoiding eye contact and not asking inappropriate questions. Explain the importance of the Elder's role in the community and the value of his or her knowledge.

- Invite the Elder to the school to meet informally with the students and staff before he or she visits the class so that the Elder can become familiar with and comfortable in the school environment.

- While the Elder is visiting the class:
  - ensure that the students listen politely and are helpful and welcoming to the Elder
  - have one of the students show the Elder around the class, the Elder's sitting area and where to find the washroom
  - have breaks during which the Elder can relax in another room if the visit is a long one
  - always supervise the students' interaction with the Elder to ensure that he or she is treated with respect and courtesy
  - provide a light lunch or snack for the Elder, such as tea, bannock and jam. Protocol usually requires that Elders are served first, followed by the students, followed by others.

Thanking an Elder

At the end of the visit, thank the Elder formally with a handshake and have the students express their appreciation for the visit. Present the Elder with a gift such as a blanket, towel set, slippers or socks, and encourage the students to present a class gift, such as a food basket containing preserves, cheese, crackers, fruit, bannock and cans of soup. This exchange of gifts is an honoured tradition arising out of the principle of reciprocity.

Welcoming Community Members

Invite guests from the Aboriginal community to the school and classroom to take part as guest speakers, performers, resource people and volunteers. Aboriginal business people, visual and performing artists, professionals, traditional teachers, athletes, storytellers and others have much to offer that will enrich programming and support cultural continuity. Consider the following guidelines when hosting Aboriginal members of the community.

- Ask contacts in the community such as liaison workers, parents and Friendship Centres to help contact appropriate visitors and to help with appropriate protocol.

- Understand that it takes time to learn about Aboriginal communities and their members. It takes time to build networks, understand the community dynamics, and honour the customs and traditions they practise.

- Take time to build a relationship with prospective guests. Invite them to visit informally or be prepared to visit them.

- Honour the principle of reciprocity when guests have completed their visits by offering an honorarium and/or a small gift of appreciation.

Welcoming the community into the classroom increases the effectiveness of teaching practices and, as a result, accountability to Aboriginal students.

story

Teacher

Shared teachings
"A traditional teacher visited our class of students with behavioural challenges and brought his teachings about the drum. Students who normally wouldn't have been able to focus for more than five minutes sat still and gave this teacher their undivided attention for half an hour. He was teaching about something that mattered to them."

Awareness of Community Protocols

Protocols are codes of etiquette that describe appropriate and respectful behaviour and ways of communicating when working with or visiting Aboriginal communities. Using proper protocols means following the customs of the people or community you are working with. Understanding and following protocols can bring about meaningful conversations that are relevant to the people involved.

Each Aboriginal community has its own protocols. Protocols can change in a community without notification, for example, when a new chief and council are elected. Protocols also change depending on whether the situation is informal or formal.

Some examples of situations that involve protocols include:
- giving tobacco (Cree) or blankets or towels (Inuit) to an Elder when seeking their knowledge or counsel
- contacting the council and explaining your intentions before visiting an Aboriginal community
- opening or closing a meeting with a prayer.

By following protocols, teachers can:
- build trusting, honest relationships
- show respect for Aboriginal cultures, values and beliefs
- allow people to speak in the voice and style of their cultural group
- create balance in the consultation and negotiation process
- improve relationships with Aboriginal communities.

Understanding protocols

When working with an Aboriginal community, it is important to understand what is important to the people who live there. When following protocols, teachers need to keep in mind the following Aboriginal beliefs and values.

Respect

Get to know the community members, and understand and honour their protocols, expectations and unique qualities without stereotyping.

Diversity

There are similarities and differences within and between Aboriginal communities, related to languages, cultures and traditions.

Oral traditions

Personal contact and dialogue are extremely important.

Time

It takes time to learn about Aboriginal communities and their members.

History

Western cultures have played a role in shaping Aboriginal communities in the past and present.

Humility

Treat each person as an equal. Titles and positions, such as teachers and school administrators, may not be considered authoritative positions in a community.

Family

Family, extended family and community obligations have a higher priority than business and other concerns.

Arranging a Visit to an Aboriginal Community

When arranging to visit an Aboriginal community, consider the following guidelines.

- Find someone who can guide you, such as an Aboriginal liaison worker, cultural advisor or another member of the community, such as a parent or teacher. Consider whether you will be covering topics that are gender-specific during your visit. If so, you should choose a female guide for female topics and a male guide for male topics.

  If you do not know anyone who can help, look on the Web site of the department of Indian and Northern Affairs Canada for a community profile. Scan the community profile for the name of an organization that has a successful working relationship with the community, and contact them for advice and information about the community dynamics.

- Educate yourself on the structure, history, protocols, values and beliefs of the Aboriginal community you will be visiting. Write down any questions you have. Your guide should be able to provide much of the information you need.

- Ask your guide to make arrangements for your visit to the community. Be prepared to share background information about yourself and the purpose of your visit.

- If you are still waiting to hear about your visit after several days, follow up informally by phone with the Aboriginal liaison worker to see how the arrangements are going. Be patient and as flexible as possible. Allow time for a response.

- If more time passes and you have not heard back, follow up with a more formal letter to the chief and council.

- If more time passes and you have not heard back, contact the local Band Office Administration by phone to explain your needs. Discuss what you would like to do on your visit and get direction on how to proceed.

Chapter 5

Learning Strategies for Aboriginal Students:
Opportunities to make learning meaningful

This chapter will help teachers to:
- use effective instructional strategies that will support the learning needs and strengths of Aboriginal students
- gain a better understanding of the unique worldviews of Aboriginal students.

The teacher's relationship with the student is at the heart of Aboriginal approaches to education. Traditionally, teachers knew each student as an individual, with unique gifts and needs. In this environment, they tailored the learning process to the student's needs as a matter of course.

Tailoring the learning process for Aboriginal students helps to engage their interest and allows them to succeed. To do this, teachers need to:
- build relationships with individual students
- gather information through conversations with students, parents and other teachers
- observe students in a variety of situations.

In Aboriginal approaches to learning, simply knowing information is not enough. Students are supported, encouraged and challenged to own their learning, to bring it into context, to make it part of their experience and to reflect on what they have learned. The strategies explored in this chapter support this kind of learning experience.

Shared wisdom

> "Touch their spirits softly with the feather of encouragement, whispering, 'You can, you will, you must, your people need you,' …"
>
> – Wilson in Gilliland 1999, p. 100

Effective Instructional Strategies

Effective instructional strategies will encourage Aboriginal students to become independent, strategic learners by:

- engaging and motivating them
- reflecting their cultures and worldviews
- helping them focus
- organizing information for ease of understanding and remembering.

Students become successful strategic learners when they are offered:

- a variety of approaches and learning materials
- appropriate support that includes modelling, guided practice and independent practice
- opportunities to transfer skills and ideas from one situation to another
- meaningful connections between skills and ideas, and real-life situations
- opportunities to be independent and show what they know
- encouragement to self-monitor and self-correct
- tools for reflecting on and assessing their learning.

Teachers often say that their Aboriginal students are quiet in class and do not participate much in large group discussions, particularly when there are only a few Aboriginal students in the classroom. Yet teachers see that Aboriginal students do participate when they feel comfortable and safe as learners.

The following types of instructional strategies can be especially effective for Aboriginal students:

- graphic organizers
- cooperative learning
- independent study
- service learning.

These strategies are effective across grade levels and subject areas, and can accommodate a range of student differences. They resonate strongly with Aboriginal students when used to support content that reflects cultural continuity. This chapter will provide a brief description of each strategy and offer sample strategies for using them with Aboriginal students.

Graphic Organizers

Graphic organizers (also known as key visuals or cognitive organizers) are formats for visually organizing information—they make students' thinking visible.

Graphic organizers reflect a holistic approach to learning by revealing not only *what* students are thinking but also *how* they are thinking as they work through learning tasks.

Students can use graphic organizers to:
- generate ideas
- record and reorganize information
- see relationships between concepts
- apply their learning
- show their thinking.

Examples of common graphic organizers include Fishbones, T-charts, Venn diagrams, P–M–I charts, K–W–L charts and Mind Maps.

Planning with graphic organizers

Graphic organizers are useful for students, but they are also a good planning tool for teachers. Using graphic organizers to plan learning activities gives teachers opportunities to become familiar with the tools and the many ways that they can be applied in the classroom.

When deciding which graphic organizer to use in a learning activity, consider the following questions.

- What type of thinking tool is best for this new concept?

- What level and type of support will best help the students?

- Is the tool developmentally appropriate for these students?

- How can the tool be modified?

- How can the tool be used interactively?

- In what other areas and ways can this tool be applied?

Using graphic organizers with students

Consider the following framework for introducing, teaching and extending the use of graphic organizers in the classroom.

Introduce
- Show examples of the new organizer, and describe its purpose and form. For example, "A T-chart is a two-column chart in the shape of a T that can be used to compare two situations."

81

Model

- Use easy or familiar material to model how to use organizers.

- Model organizers on the board, overhead or chart paper, using a think-aloud format. Use colours to enhance memory and create meaning.

- Give explicit oral directions, explanations and reflections when modelling.

Guided practice

- Give students opportunities to practise using the format with easy material.

- Coach students at selected points in the process.

- Create opportunities for students to collaborate and discuss with each other.

Reflect

- Share final products; discuss what worked and what did not, and give students an opportunity to revise information.

Practise

- Provide students with many opportunities to practise using graphic organizers.

- Make templates of several different kinds of organizers available. Encourage students to choose the most appropriate organizer for a task, and to design their own versions.

Transfer

- Use graphic organizers across a range of learning situations and content areas.

Evaluate and extend use

- Encourage students to evaluate which organizers work best for them and in which learning situations.

- Encourage students to use a variety of organizers independently in a variety of learning tasks, such as note taking, researching and studying.

Fishbone

The Fishbone can be used to explore cause and effect, to analyze the results of an event (for example, in history), as a planning tool for creating an action plan, or as a review of information learned.

The head of the Fishbone names the issue or idea or outcome to be focused on, with causes, events or key concepts listed on the backbone, and supporting ideas listed on the ribs.

Teacher story

Exploring Aboriginal perspectives of the land
"I used the Fishbone organizer with my Grade 8 regular and academic support students.

When studying the geography of North America, I used a cultural infusion approach to learning by having students consider Aboriginal perspectives of the land. I had in a guest who presented three lessons. The lessons included a personal story demonstrating connections to the land and one's place of growing up, and quotations on the land from a variety of Aboriginal groups.

Students viewed a video focusing on the interconnectedness of people and the land from four global indigenous perspectives, including the Lubicon of Alberta. The final lesson included a story and visuals on sacred spaces and the spiritual component of the land.

In the class following the sessions with the guest presenter, students were given 'sticky notes' to write down as many things as they could remember from the lessons, one idea per note. Then they sat with a partner, compared sticky notes and grouped their responses into larger categories. Students used different coloured stickies to identify different categories. Once they had done this, I introduced the Fishbone organizer and students worked in pairs to transfer the information from the sticky notes to a single sheet.

The Fishbone organizer helped me to assess what students had learned and helped the students to solidify what they had learned."

The example follows.

(continued)

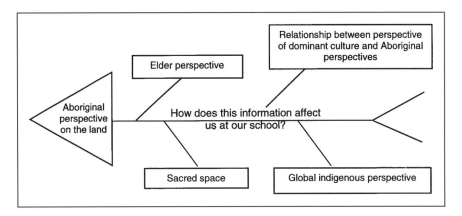

For a blackline master of this graphic organizer, see *Appendix 9: Fishbone*.

T-chart

T-charts help students organize their information and ideas, and see relationships between pieces of information. T-charts can have two, three or more columns.

T-charts can be valuable tools for describing or visualizing. They can also be used to compare and contrast different issues or situations, for example, a looks like/sounds like/feels like chart.

story

Teacher

The sound of a moose

"My Grade 3 students had great fun using empty tin cans to make moose calls as part of a sound unit in science. We removed the top lid and then made a hole in the bottom lid. We knotted one end of a piece of string and pulled it through the hole and out the open end of the can. To make the sound of a moose we wet the string and pulled two fingers down the length of the string.

The students tried out several different sizes of cans and created a T-chart to record how the size of the can affected the sound each can produced.

The students observed that the biggest can produced the loudest call with the lowest pitch. The class consensus was that the big can sounded like a father moose, the middle-size can sounded like a mother moose and the smallest can sounded like a baby moose!

This is what we recorded on our class T-chart."

(continued)

How does the size of can affect the moose call?	
Looks like:	**Sounds like:**
Small cylinder: tomato soup can	*Soft "moowah"*
Medium cylinder: beef stew can	*Medium pitch*
Large cylinder: coffee can	*Low loud pitch*

For a blackline master of this graphic organizer, see *Appendix 10: T-chart*.

Venn diagram

A Venn diagram includes two or more interlocking circles that can be used to compare two or more objects, concepts or ideas in a way that shows both similarities and differences. This tool helps students organize information and see relationships.

Venn diagrams can be used after such activities as reading text, listening to a speaker or viewing a film. They can also be expanded to three or more circles in order to compare a number of issues or concepts.

Teacher story

Using Venn diagrams

"I had my Grade 4 class read the children's book, *The Journal of Etienne Mercier* by Métis author David Bouchard. Students created a Venn diagram comparing the cultural traditions of their lives with those described in the story."

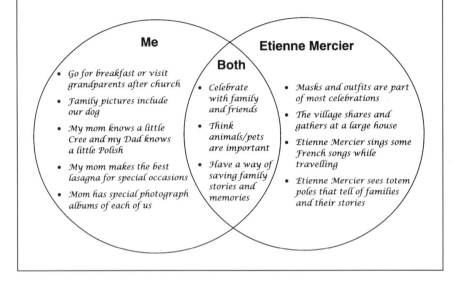

Me

- Go for breakfast or visit grandparents after church
- Family pictures include our dog
- My mom knows a little Cree and my Dad knows a little Polish
- My mom makes the best lasagna for special occasions
- Mom has special photograph albums of each of us

Both

- Celebrate with family and friends
- Think animals/pets are important
- Have a way of saving family stories and memories

Etienne Mercier

- Masks and outfits are part of most celebrations
- The village shares and gathers at a large house
- Etienne Mercier sings some French songs while travelling
- Etienne Mercier sees totem poles that tell of families and their stories

For a blackline master of this graphic organizer, see *Appendix 11: Venn Diagram.*

P–M–I chart

Students can use Plus, Minus and Interesting (P–M–I) charts to compare and contrast situations, ideas or positions. P–M–I charts give students a format for organizing information, and evaluating their knowledge and ideas. Students can use this tool to collect data and organize information to make informed decisions.

Why we should learn our Aboriginal language

Plus	Minus	Interesting
• *You can talk to Elders* • *You can appreciate true meaning of stories and songs* • *You will have new understanding of traditional beliefs that can only be understood by speaking the language* • *You can teach your own children the language!*	• *Learning another language is hard work and takes time* • *Only a few people speak my Aboriginal language*	• *Many Aboriginal parents found their first days in English-speaking schools difficult. They didn't want their own children to experience this struggle so they decided not to use their Aboriginal language at home.* • *Many people in the world speak two or more languages. Learning more than one language can help you become a better learner.*

What do I think? Why?

Now that I have considered all the information, my thoughts on this topic are:

I know it will be hard work to learn Cree but I want to learn stories and songs from my grandmother. I think learning my language will help me understand better what it means to be First Nations.

For a blackline master of this graphic organizer, see *Appendix 12: P–M–I Chart.*

Place Mat

Students can use the Place Mat to organize details for writing, and share information and ideas about a story. They can also use it to display a table of contents for a project or portfolio, or compare and contrast four items.

The Place Mat can also be used by a small group to collect and organize information collaboratively, and build consensus. Consider the following type of activity.

- In groups of three or four, students divide their section of the place mat into three sections: Plus, Minus and Interesting.

- They write about an issue for one minute in their Plus section.

- Then they rotate the mat and write in someone else's Plus section.

- They repeat the process until they get their own section back.

- They repeat the process with the Minus and Interesting sections. Finally, the group writes their consensus, or shared ideas, in the centre section of the place mat.

The Moccasin Goalie

Setting

Plot

This story takes place during the winter in "the old days on the Prairies" in a small town called Willow.

This is a true story about a young boy named Danny who cannot wear boots or skates because of a physical disability. He wears moccasins. At first he is not allowed to play hockey without skates. When the regular player gets hurt Danny gets to play in his moccasins.

Characters

*Anita
Marcel
Petou*

*Moccasin Danny
Bingo (a dog)*

Title: *The Moccasin Goalie*

Author: *William Roy Brownridge*

Review

This story is about playing hockey. What makes it interesting is the fact that moccasins make it possible for a boy with disabilities to play the sport. The story makes you think about how moccasins are one example of the gifts Aboriginal people have given to Canada.

For a blackline master of this graphic organizer, see *Appendix 13: Place Mat*.

K–W–L chart (Ogle 1986)

K–W–L is a brainstorming strategy. It is also known as a know–wonder–learn or What I know–What I want to know–What I learned chart. This tool encourages students to ask questions and to make a link between what they know and what they need to learn about a topic. The K–W–L chart helps students to organize information and find a starting point for other tasks such as research projects and assignments.

K–W–L can be done individually, in small groups or as a class activity, with the teacher recording the ideas.

Teacher story

Using K–W–L charts

"I find this chart most useful when I'm beginning a lesson. I'll present a topic in the form of a question such as 'How did the buffalo help to sustain the lives of prairie tribes?'

Students then identify what they 'know' about the topic. Then they're given the opportunity to ask the 'I wonder' questions. Finally, they move to the 'learn' portion of the chart. Here they can suggest places or resources they can use to continue their learning on this topic."

How did the buffalo help to sustain the lives of prairie tribes?

K I Know	W I Wonder	L I will Look/Learn from
• buffalo skins were used for clothing and shelter • pemmican was made from buffalo meat • buffalo were killed in large numbers by running over a cliff	• What were the other parts of the buffalo used for? • Were there other ways to kill buffalo? • What jobs were done by the women? By the men? • How often did they have to go hunting? • How long would it take to skin a buffalo?	• textbook • Internet search—buffalo, Cree, Blackfoot • field trip—Head Smashed In Buffalo Jump • guest speaker: First Nations person • stories

For a blackline master of this graphic organizer, see *Appendix 14: K–W–L Chart.*

Mind map

Mind mapping was developed in the early 1970s by British author and brain researcher Tony Buzan. It is an easy way to represent ideas using keywords, colours and imagery. The nonlinear format helps students generate and organize ideas, record a large amount of information on one piece of paper, and show connections between ideas. This tool integrates logical and imaginative thinking, and provides an overview of what students know and think about a particular topic.

Webs are simple mind maps. Adding pictures, colours and keywords transforms them into a more powerful learning, memory and idea-generating tool.

Teacher story

Using mind maps

"I've used a mind map to help students learn about the Riel Rebellions (1870 and 1885), which are key to the development of western Canada and to furthering the alienation of Quebec within Canada. Because the Riel incidents can be viewed from multiple perspectives, it is useful for students to use a mind map to pull this information together. Mind maps can help students explore the tension between ideas while noting their interconnectedness. For example, a mind map on the Riel Rebellions allows the position of the Canadian government in reaction to US foreign policy to be represented alongside the relationship between the Métis and First Nations people."

The Riel Rebellions (1870, 1885)

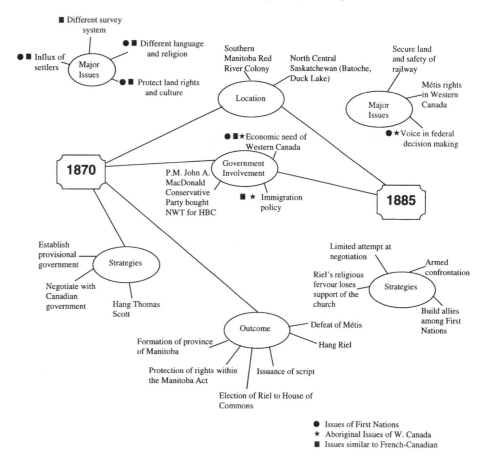

■ Different survey system

● ■ Different language and religion

● ■ Influx of settlers

Major Issues

● ■ Protect land rights and culture

Southern Manitoba Red River Colony

North Central Saskatchewan (Batoche, Duck Lake)

Location

Secure land and safety of railway

Major Issues

Métis rights in Western Canada

● ★ Voice in federal decision making

● ■ ★ Economic need of Western Canada

Government Involvement

P.M. John A. MacDonald Conservative Party bought NWT for HBC

■ ★ Immigration policy

1870

1885

Establish provisional government

Strategies

Negotiate with Canadian government

Hang Thomas Scott

Limited attempt at negotiation

Armed confrontation

Riel's religious fervour loses support of the church

Strategies

Build allies among First Nations

Defeat of Métis

Hang Riel

Outcome

Formation of province of Manitoba

Protection of rights within the Manitoba Act

Issuance of script

Election of Riel to House of Commons

● Issues of First Nations
★ Aboriginal Issues of W. Canada
■ Issues similar to French-Canadian

Cooperative Learning

Cooperative learning, where students work in small groups to complete tasks or projects, is an effective strategy to use with Aboriginal students because it reflects the sense of cooperation and community that is a vital aspect of Aboriginal cultures.

Use cooperative learning to:
- increase students' respect for and understanding of each other's abilities, interests, needs and differences
- encourage students to take responsibility for their own learning.

Cooperative learning tasks are structured so that each group member contributes to the completion of the task. Success is based on the performance of the group rather than on the performance of individual students, another strong reflection of Aboriginal cultural values.

Cooperative learning activities range from simple to complex. Beginning with simple activities allows students to develop the skills they need to participate effectively in more complex activities.

Simple cooperative activities include Think–Pair–Share, Inside/Outside Circles and the Three-step Interview. More complex activities include Jigsaw and Group Investigation.

Setting the stage

- Discuss and model collaborative skills, such as listening, allowing others to speak, asking for help when needed, reaching consensus and completing a task within the allotted time. Students need opportunities to practise these skills, and to receive feedback and reinforcement.

- Teach basic routines for classroom management, including forming groups quickly and quietly, maintaining appropriate noise levels, inviting others to join the group, treating all students with respect and helping or encouraging peers.

Consider the following tips for organizing groups.

- Keep groups small—two to five members is best (the larger the group, the more skills are required).

- Create diverse groups—this allows everyone to learn from each other's differences.

- Structure tasks or projects to ensure that success depends on each group member being responsible for some part of the task.

- Initially, group students and assign roles within each group.

- Encourage on-task behaviour by scanning groups, using proximity and friendly reminders, sitting and watching a group for a while, revisiting expectations and, when necessary, reteaching expectations.

- Ensure that individual students are aware of their roles and responsibilities within the group. Post a list of roles or give students cards describing specific roles.

- Allow students time to evaluate the cooperative learning process, both individually and as a group.

Think–pair–share

In think–pair–share, the teacher poses a topic or question. Students think privately about the question for a given amount of time, usually one to three minutes. Each student then pairs with a partner to discuss the question, allowing students to clarify their thoughts. Next, each pair has an opportunity to share their answers with the whole class.

Think–pair–share is a cooperative learning strategy that provides opportunities for students to:

- participate
- learn from others
- make connections.

story

Teacher

Using think–pair–share
"When I have a question that requires thoughtfulness on the part of the student, I use think–pair–share. It gives students time to reflect on the question first, then broaden their understanding by sharing with a partner. For example, I would use it with questions like:
- Should the Métis have asked for Riel to return in 1885?
- How would the demise of the buffalo foreshadow the difficulties of the Plains people?
- Why does the director use flashbacks in the movie *Smoke Signals*?
- What does the reader learn about Métis poet Gregory Scofield's sense of identity from his poem *Policy of the Dispossessed*?"

Inside/Outside Circles

This strategy places students facing each other in two circles, one within the other. It works best with six or more students, half in each circle.

Inside/Outside Circles facilitate dialogue between students, which helps with community building at the beginning of term. It is an effective strategy for introducing movement and variety into a lesson. It works best with engaging questions that have a range of possible answers.

To use Inside/Outside Circles, consider the following.

- Write a question on the board and give the students a minute to think about their response.

- Then have the people in the inside circle tell their partners in the outside how they would answer the question or solve the problem, saying "pass" when they are finished.

- Then, the person on the outside takes a turn answering the question.

- When both students in a pair have had a turn, rotate the outer or inner circle for a new pairing.

Teacher story

> **Using Inside/Outside Circles**
> "I like to use Inside/Outside Circles when I have a question that has a range of possible responses, for example:
> - How did Canada benefit from the Riel Rebellions?
> - How has the use of treaties with First Nations peoples contributed to Canada's national identity?
> - How have animals contributed to the survival of First Nations peoples?"

Brainstorming

Brainstorming is an effective technique for generating ideas and creating interest and enthusiasm for new concepts or topics. Brainstorming is a creative form of list making, which creates opportunities for students to come up with as many ideas about a topic as they can.

Students can use brainstorming as a starting point for more complex tasks, such as essay outlines or mind maps.

Tips for Brainstorming

- Establish ground rules. For example, accept all ideas without judgement, everyone participates, focus on quantity rather than quality.

- Establish the purpose. For example, brainstorm to come up with a fun theme for a class party.

- Establish the limits for brainstorming. For example, generate as many ideas as possible in five minutes, or go for 25 really good ideas, or three ideas from each group.

- Revise the list. For example, cross out ideas that are not feasible, combine similar ideas, put ideas in a logical sequence.

To make a decision from a brainstormed list:
- give each student three coloured stick-on dots and have students cast a vote for their favourite choices by putting dots beside them
- use a process of elimination to reach a consensus on the final choice.

Brainstorm

Topic: *Activities for celebrating Aboriginal Day*

Goal *Ideas for activities for Aboriginal Day*   Time limit *10* minutes

Why am I doing this?

☑ to generate ideas   ☑ to make decisions

☑ to assess prior knowledge   ❑ to review information

1. ~~*dancing*~~
2. *cook Aboriginal foods for feast*★
3. *round-dance*
4. *pow-wow dancers*
5. *Aboriginal guest speaker*
6. *Aboriginal games*★
7. *Aboriginal author book fair*
8. *Aboriginal music*
9. *Aboriginal craft fair*★
10. ~~*feast*~~

Reflect and revise

☑ Are any ideas similar? If yes, combine similar ideas.

❑ Do all ideas fit the topic? If no, cross out ideas that don't fit.

☑ Star your three ideas.

Form reproduced with permission from Edmonton Public Schools, *Thinking Tools for Kids: Practical Organizers* (Edmonton, AB: Edmonton Public Schools, 1999), p. 167.

For a blackline master of this graphic organizer, see *Appendix 15: Brainstorm.*

Graffiti

Graffiti is a brainstorming process that encourages everyone to contribute. To use Graffiti, consider the following.

- Organize students into groups of three or four.

- Give each group a large piece of paper with a topic (the same or different for each group) written in the centre.

- Give students one minute to think, then 60 to 90 seconds to write their ideas on the paper individually but simultaneously. Add interest by using coloured markers. Younger students can draw images.

- Tell students not to worry if they have the same response as someone else—if two or more of them write the same thing, that probably means the concept is important.

- Then, have the students stand and move, as a group, to a different piece of paper.

- Repeat the process until every group has visited every sheet of paper.

At the end of the process, each group will have the collective wisdom of the class on their sheet of paper.

Teacher story

Using Graffiti for brainstorming

"Graffiti lets my students provide a visual expression of a topic. We were going to read the novel, *My Name is Seepeetza*, the experience of a girl in residential school, so I wanted to start out by finding what my students knew about the topic. The topic was 'The effect of residential schools on today's First Nations communities.'

I laid out four large sheets of paper, and wrote the following headings on them, one per sheet: Funding and education, Church-operated, Limited contact with home, and Residential schools were in place from the 1870s to 1980s.

Then I divided the students into four groups. Each group gathered around one of the sheets of paper, and when I gave the signal, they began writing whatever they felt was appropriate to that heading. After a couple of minutes I had them rotate to the next sheet and do the same process. I continued until all the students had an opportunity to write on all four topics.

Once they were finished, we looked at the responses as a group. We looked at the frequency of ideas and the range of opinions. I raised questions with the students that had them:
- consider responses that affirmed what they knew
- identify what might be unsubstantiated points of view
- identify thoughts that might lead to new perspectives or new questions to be explored."

Walk About

Walk About is a strategy patterned on cross-pollination. After the class has worked in groups on a strategy such as Place Mat or Graffiti, one member from each group moves on to another group, carrying ideas from the first group with him or her.

Walk About builds interest, individual accountability, physical movement and variety into the learning process.

To select the student who will move, have the original groups letter or number off, then all the "ones" or "As" move on to the next group.

story

Teacher

Using a Walk About

"I read the *Journal of Etienne Mercier* by Métis author David Bouchard to my students. I broke students into groups of four and gave each group a Place Mat with four sections with the headings: Government structures, Ceremonies, Animals and Vocabulary. I gave the students about 10 minutes to complete their Place Mats as a group. Then we did a Walk About. One student from each group took their Place Mat to another group and shared their ideas."

Three-step Interview

The Three-step Interview encourages students to share their thinking, ask questions and take notes.

Use the Three-step Interview to:
- problem solve, so that each student has the opportunity to say how he or she would approach a problem
- identify key ideas in a group report
- discuss a recently read book.

To use the Three-step Interview, consider the following.

- Place students into groups of three and assign each student a letter: A, B or C.

- Assign each letter a role: A=Interviewer, B=Interviewee, C=Reporter.

- Student A interviews student B while C takes notes. The roles then rotate after each interview.

- When each student has taken each role, have students share key information they recorded as the Reporter.

story

Teacher

Using interviews

"I wanted my students to better understand the concept of role models. I gave each of my students a short biography of a First Nations or Métis role model. Then I broke the students into groups of three. After reading their biographies, the students shared information about what they had read, then followed this with the Three-step Interview. The interview focused on what makes that person a good role model."

97

Three-step Interview

Interview One: Jasmine

Susan Aglukark is an Inuit. She was born in Churchill, Manitoba in 1967. She grew up in Arviat, Nunavut. She is a famous singer who sings in English and in her traditional language Inuktitut. Her songs contain images of her culture. She is a role model because she stays true to her culture. She also speaks to youth and tells them to stay in school. She is a good role model because she sets a good example.

Interview Two: Jesse

George Littlechild is a Métis. He is part Plains Cree and part White. He was born in Edmonton, Alberta in 1958. Even though he was raised by a foster family because his parents were deceased, he still honours his Aboriginal roots. He does this through his paintings. He makes a good role model because he is proud of his heritage and his art is exhibited in galleries and museums all over the world.

Interview Three: Jordan

Joseph Francis Dion is a Plains Cree who was born near Onion Lake on July 2, 1888. During the 1930s, when he was living by Kehewin Reserve, he became involved with efforts to ease the plight of the Métis in Alberta. Even though he was treaty, he was concerned about the poverty and living conditions of the Métis people. He worked with concerned others to form l'Association des Métis d'Alberta et des Territories du Nord-Ouest. This later became known as the Métis Association of Alberta. This group worked to bring Métis issues to the public. He sacrificed time with his family. He is a role model because he put the needs of Métis people before himself.

Round Robin: Key ideas from interviews

Aboriginal role models can be of any age, gender or time period. There are different mediums to present positive Aboriginal values such as music, art and politics. Role-models think about helping others.

For a blackline master to support this activity, see *Appendix 16: Three-step Interview.*

Jigsaw

In the Jigsaw strategy, students become "experts" in one or two concepts or pieces of information and then share their expertise with students in their home group. At the completion of the activity, all the pieces of information fit together like a jigsaw puzzle to become a whole.

To use the Jigsaw strategy, consider the following.

- Divide a concept or topic—for example, fractions or northern ecosystems—into several areas.

- Place students in home groups of four or six. One approach to consider is to have pairs of students working together on one topic, teaming students who are weaker with students who are stronger to create a natural peer tutoring situation.

- Number or letter off group members. Assign all As to one or two areas: expressing fractions in lowest terms, for example, or reading an article about boreal forest management. Give Bs, Cs and Ds, and so on, different assignments.

- Have all As meet to share what they have learned about their area. Bs, Cs and Ds and so on, also meet.

- Experts then return to their home group to share all that they know and all that they have learned from the other experts in their area.

Teacher story

Using a Jigsaw

"After over 300 years of being a fur trade company, the Hudson Bay Company made the decision to no longer sell furs because of international pressure. I thought this was a really relevant issue for many of my students, and that it was important for them to reflect on the question: should foreign countries be able to pressure other countries to change their practices?

I showed students the CBC News in Review on this topic and then used the Jigsaw strategy to structure their discussion. After breaking the students into groups, I gave each group member a letter. In their letter groups, students read short articles offering a perspective on the fur trade. That is, all the As read an article on clubbing seals, the Bs read a short article on trapping and the northern economy, and so on.

Once they had discussed the articles in their 'expert' groups, they returned to their home groups to share what they had learned. Then we discussed the issue as a whole class."

Four Corners

In the Four Corners strategy, students "vote with their feet." Each corner of the classroom, or cleared space in the classroom, represents one of four answers to a question or four points of view about an issue. Students move to the corner of the room that best reflects their point of view about an issue or idea.

Four Corners encourages students to think creatively and evaluate their ideas.

To use the Four Corners strategy, consider the following.

- Begin with a statement, issue or question. For example, "Which organ—heart, brain, liver, lungs—is most important?" or "Smoking should not be allowed in restaurants."

- Identify four corners that correspond to the statement or question, for example "Heart, Brain, Liver, Lungs" or "Strongly Agree, Agree, Disagree, Strongly Disagree."

- Students choose the corner that most accurately expresses their opinion, response or point of view.

- The students move to their chosen corner.

- If others move to the same corner, they share with each other why they chose that corner.

- Students should be prepared to share the reasons for their choice with the whole group.

Teacher story

Using Four Corners
"I found a number of articles about Native Land Claims and logging on crown land. The different articles reflected different perspectives including lumber companies, forestry officials, environmentalists and Aboriginal people. Students used the articles to make informed opinions in response to the statement, "The government should have total access to land for economic development." Each of the students moved to one of four corners to indicate their level of agreement with the statement. They discussed their positions with other class members who chose the same corner and then they presented their case to the whole class. It was interesting to hear the different perspectives. It created a valuable opportunity for students to reflect on one another's viewpoints."

Independent Study

In traditional Aboriginal cultures, survival depended on making independent judgements, so learning to take responsibility for one's behaviour was paramount. Responsibility for one's behaviour fosters motivation to attain a given goal. In this context, independence means recognizing and making good use of one's power. It does not mean working in social isolation (Brendtro, Brokenleg and Van Bockern 1990).

Independent study can facilitate the development of student responsibility. Independent study is an individualized learning experience in which students select a topic focus, define problems or questions, gather and analyze information, apply skills and create a product to show what they have learned.[12] It is a way to create opportunities for Aboriginal students to undertake learning that is meaningful to them.

Independent study projects can encourage students to:
- gather, analyze and report information
- develop in-depth understanding of specific content areas
- make connections between content and real-life applications.[12]

Regular student–teacher interaction, whether structured conferences or casual conversations, are essential for successful independent study. The teacher's role is to:
- keep in touch
- help with problem solving
- provide direction
- open up new areas for exploration and production
- give encouragement
- introduce, teach and/or reinforce needed skills.[12]

This learning strategy reflects the experiential, practical, try-it-for-yourself aspect of Aboriginal education. It is most effective for students who have a high degree of self-direction. A mastery of basic research skills is a prerequisite to successful independent study.

Basics[12]

A successful independent study project requires:
- cooperative teacher–student planning of what will be studied and how it will be shared
- alternative ideas for gathering and processing information
- multiple resources that are readily available
- teacher interaction
- time designated specifically for working and conferencing
- working and storage space
- opportunities for sharing, feedback and evaluation
- recognition from other students of expertise gained and the finished product
- established evaluation criteria.

---

12. Adapted from *Change for Children: Ideas and Activities for Individualizing Learning* (Revised Edition) (pp. 169, 170) by S. N. Kaplan, J. B. Kaplan, S. K. Madsen and B. T. Gould. © 1980 by Scott, Foresman and Company. Used by permission of Pearson Education, Inc.

Independent study plans

As students are planning, encourage them to:

- select topics or issues that motivate them
- brainstorm and discuss possible questions
- identify key questions to pursue and answer
- develop plans and timelines
- locate and use multiple resources
- decide how to use what they learn to create products
- share findings with classmates
- evaluate the process, products and use of time
- explore possibilities that could extend their studies into new areas of learning.[12]

Students can use a graphic organizer, such as the sample on the following page, to plan their study.

© Alberta Education, Alberta, Canada

Why is this an important question?

There are various stories describing a Métis flag with an infinity sign on a red or blue background. As a Métis person I want to know why two different colours are used and the history behind each colour.

(Rationale)

What is my critical question?

Why are there two different background colours for the Métis flag?

How can I show my learning?

An oral presentation of story about Métis flag. Have flags to show.

(Product/format)

Where can I look for information and answers?

- *Métis Elders*
- *Sweetgrass and Windspeaker newspapers*
- *Métis organizations*
- *Internet*

(Sources)

When will I do **what**?

Sept. 1–7	*Check Internet sources*
Sept. 8–14	*Talk to Native liaison worker to get names of Métis Elders. Take them a gift (tobacco if appropriate) and ask permission to interview them.*
Sept. 15–21	*Check newspaper articles.*
Sept. 22–28	*Write report and get flags or draw them.*
Sept. 29	*Do presentation for Grade 10 Aboriginal Studies class.*

(Timeline)

Who ...

... has information? *school library, Internet, Native liaison worker, Métis Elders, newspapers, Friendship Centre, Métis organizations*

... will review and discuss my project? *My teacher, classmates, Native liaison worker, Métis Elders if they want*

... will be my final audience? *Grade 10 Aboriginal Studies class*

Form reproduced with permission from Edmonton Public Schools, *Think Again: Thinking Tools for Grades 6 to 10* (Edmonton, AB: Edmonton Public Schools, 2003), p. 95.

story

Teacher

> **Setting up an independent study**
>
> "One of my students was interested in learning about dislocated people in Canada. I thought it was a really intriguing question, so I supported the student's interest by setting her up in an independent study. She decided to focus on Davis Inlet and the impact relocation had on its people.
>
> After some initial discussion, we came up with the research question: Would the people of Davis Inlet meet the UN criteria of refugee? Neither of us had an answer to that question, but thought it was worth exploring.
>
> We decided she should use several sources of information to gather diverse perspectives, including the United Nations Web site, as well as the CBC News in Review on Davis Inlet. As well, I knew that some of the youth from Davis Inlet had attended an Aboriginal treatment centre nearby – so I thought she might find it interesting to talk to one of the counsellors there to get a different perspective. I taught her how to create questions based on Bloom's taxonomy, to use when she talked to the counsellor.
>
> Evaluation of the project involved multiple assessments, including a PowerPoint presentation and a rubric assessing the quality of the questions she created for the counsellor at the treatment centre."

For a blackline master to support independent research, see *Appendix 17: Independent Study Planner*.

Service Learning

Service learning can benefit both students and their community—in and beyond the school. In service learning, students provide a service to the community and in doing so, learn more about their community and about themselves while practising skills such as goal setting, problem solving and planning.

For Aboriginal students, service learning reflects the commitment to community that is traditionally a vital aspect of Aboriginal cultures.

Service learning benefits students and communities by:[13]
- building connections among students, their schools and their communities
- improving school climate as students work together in positive ways
- showing the community a positive image of youth, leading to stronger support for students and schools
- creating greater awareness of community needs and concerns
- increasing community capacity to address key issues.

Service learning encourages students to:[13]
- strengthen academic knowledge and skills by applying them to real situations
- build positive relationships and work with a variety of people
- discover new interests and abilities
- set goals and work to achieve them
- work cooperatively, and also learn the importance of individual responsibility
- take on leadership roles
- learn the value of helping and caring for others.

Teacher story

Using service learning
"Contributing to the community is very important in Aboriginal communities, so my students were quite excited about undertaking a service learning project. They wanted it to be meaningful, so they decided to plan an Aboriginal fine-arts celebration for National Aboriginal Days, an event widely celebrated by Aboriginal peoples.

The students were responsible for all of it, including identifying a program, contacting Aboriginal artists from the community, developing an advertising strategy, arranging for a ceremonial opening and greeting, taking care of traditional people and guests as they arrived, and acknowledging those who contributed to the performance.

It was a wonderful learning experience for the kids to organize such an event for the community!"

13. Adapted with permission from Lions Clubs International, *Skills for Adolescence: Changes and Challenges* (4th edition) (Oak Brook, IL: Lions Clubs International Foundation, 2003), p. 4.

Sample service learning projects[14]

Goal: To make school a positive place for everyone.

Possible projects

- Create posters with positive messages on friendship, cooperation, cross-cultural understanding, school spirit and other topics.
- Start schoolwide campaigns to eliminate put-downs. Make posters, organize noon-hour events and involve school staff.
- Begin campaigns using posters, buttons and bulletin boards to encourage students to strive toward higher academic achievement. Develop special awards for improvement. Organize workshops and tutoring programs.
- Make information available about scholarships and other opportunities for Aboriginal learners.
- Plan appreciation days for school volunteers.
- Plan appreciation days for school staff.

Goal: To contribute to young families in the community.

Possible projects

- Plan special parties for children in daycare.
- Teach simple crafts based on Aboriginal traditions to children in after-school programs.
- Read Aboriginal literature to children in elementary school.
- Organize on-site babysitting services for special parent and community meetings held at the school.

For more information about service learning, see pages 94–100 of Alberta Education's *Kindergarten to Grade 9 Health and Life Skills Guide to Implementation* (2002).

Turning service projects into service learning

Service learning is a way of taking the classroom to the community. It introduces analysis, planning and evaluation into community service projects. The experience will help students develop a sense of community and purpose, as well as a real understanding of local needs and issues. Students who complete all of the following steps of service learning will realize that their actions make a difference.

Step 1: Prepare

With teacher guidance, students:

- decide which needs in the community and the school they want to address
- list questions they have about the issues involved and research the answers

---

14. Adapted with permission from Lions Clubs International, *Skills for Adolescence: Service Learning* (4th edition) (Oak Brook, IL: Lions Clubs International Foundation, 2003), pp. 64–65.

- develop an understanding of why their project is significant and how it will benefit their community
- define desired outcomes and goals
- consider how they can collaborate with parents and community partners to address these needs
- develop a project (or projects) that responds to authentic needs in the school or community.

Choosing a Service Learning Project

Identified Need: _____

1. List reasons this is an important need for the class to address.
   _____
   _____
   _____

2. What is one short-term project the class could do to address this need?
   _____
   _____
   _____

3. What is needed for this project? (Think about expenses, materials, adult help, transportations.)
   _____
   _____
   _____

4. What challenges or barriers might keep this project from being successful?
   _____
   _____
   _____

5. What are *two* long-term projects the class might carry out to address this need?
   _____
   _____
   _____

Adapted with permission from Lions Clubs International, *Skills for Adolescence: Service Learning* (4th edition) (Oak Brook, IL: Lions Clubs International Foundation, 2003), pp. 48–49.

Step 2: Plan

With teacher guidance to ensure that the learning provides meaningful service and real consequences, students can:
- develop a plan and timeline
- take responsibility for their part of the project
- consider ways to communicate effectively with the school, parents and community about the project, to encourage others to participate
- consider possible challenges and roadblocks, and how they might be overcome.

107

Making It Happen

Service Learning Project Plan

1. The need we will address: _____
   _____

2. A brief description of our project: _____
   _____
   _____
   _____

3. Our project goals: _____
   _____
   _____
   _____
   _____

4. Our committee: _____
   _____
   _____
   _____

Jobs to be done	Who will do them?	Timelines

Adapted with permission from Lions Clubs International, *Skills for Adolescence: Service Learning* (4th edition) (Oak Brook, IL: Lions Clubs International Foundation, 2003), p. 51.

Step 3: Put the plan into action

As students put their plan into action, teachers need to:

- ensure that students assume as much responsibility as possible
- ensure that the service learning project happens in an environment that is safe, and that the project creates opportunities for mistakes and successes
- involve parents and pre-screened community volunteers, and monitor performance and safety on a regular basis.

Step 4: Review, reflect and demonstrate

It is essential that at the end of service learning projects, students have opportunities to privately and publicly reflect on what they have contributed and learned through the project. Students need opportunities to:

- acknowledge and celebrate everyone's participation
- reinforce what they have learned through the service learning project by demonstrating their mastery of skills and new insights by reporting to their classmates, families and communities, writing articles or letters to local newspapers about community issues, or using what they have learned to develop future projects in the community.

Reflecting on Our Service Learning

1. What skills did the class use to carry out this project?

_____

_____

_____

_____

_____

_____

2. What was accomplished through this project?

_____

_____

_____

_____

_____

_____

3. What can we do to improve our next project?

_____

_____

_____

_____

_____

_____

Adapted with permission from Lions Clubs International, *Skills for Adolescence: Service Learning* (4th edition) (Oak Brook, IL: Lions Clubs International Foundation, 2003), p. 52.

For blackline masters that support service learning, see *Appendix 18: Choosing a Service Learning Project, Appendix 19: Making It Happen*, and *Appendix 20: Reflecting on Our Service Learning*.

Chapter 6

Assessment:
Authentic reflections of important learnings

This chapter will help teachers to:
- understand the cultural implications of classroom assessment and grading practices
- recognize the ways that culturally appropriate assessment can support the learning success of Aboriginal students
- develop multiple approaches to assessment that will support the learning needs and strengths of Aboriginal students.

Rethinking Assessment

While the purpose of traditional assessment, and marking and grading practices has been to sort, select and justify, current thought about assessment and current research on the relationship between assessment and learning now point to a different purpose—assessment for learning.

The focus on assessment for learning recognizes that effective assessment is not removed from the learning experience, but is embedded in authentic learning activities based on higher-order thinking skills, such as problem solving and analysis. Assessment for learning recognizes that students can be motivated to take increased responsibility for their own learning when they experience assessment as an integral part of the learning process.

Assessment for learning is authentic and based on brain-based research. It also requires a high degree of assessment literacy, meaning that teachers need to understand how to use multiple types of assessment strategies.

Authentic assessment
Authentic assessments reflect real learning that is meaningful to students. Authentic assessments:
- reflect understandings and abilities that matter in life
- are educational and engaging
- grow out of curriculum studies and are designed to do much more than "shake out a grade"
- present real-life, interdisciplinary situations

- pose complex, open-ended challenges that require integration of knowledge and skills
- often result in performances or presentations.

Assessment literacy

Assessment literacy includes:

- understanding and using multiple assessment methods, to ensure that the information gathered about student learning is complete and accurate, and that individual students have the opportunity to demonstrate their learning in a variety of ways
- communicating assessment criteria and results effectively
- involving students as partners in the assessment process.

Brain-based research

The "brain-compatible" classroom provides five elements that facilitate learning (Chapman 1993). Brain-compatible or brain-based assessment pays attention to the same five elements. These elements include the following.

- **Trust and belonging**—Familiar environments, practice assessments and second chances all provide the comfort that students need during assessment activities.

- **Meaningful content** and **enriched environment**—Assessment activities are chosen because they promote learning, not because they are easy to score.

- **Intelligent choices**—Students have some choice about how they are assessed and all students are not required to show their achievement in the same way.

- **Adequate time**—Students need time to become familiar with assessment activities. They also need sufficient time to demonstrate their learning. Time-limited assessment is only valid when time is a critical element in the learning.

The new focus on authentic, brain-based assessments is a welcome development for Aboriginal students and their teachers.

The principles of authentic assessment and the principles of Aboriginal education share a number of common approaches and perspectives. The best practices fostered by assessment for learning effectively support the learning strengths and needs of Aboriginal students.

Culture and Assessment

Aboriginal students may bring a set of life experiences and responses to the classroom that are significantly different than those of most non-Aboriginal students. These learner characteristics determine the instructional and assessment strategies that will be the most effective for Aboriginal students. Aligning assessment approaches to match students' life experiences and culturally-based responses ensures that assessment practices are fair, inclusive and authentic, and that they contribute to student learning and overall sense of connection to learning.

Coming from cultures that value oral and observational learning, Aboriginal students may not be as comfortable with paper and pencil assessments as they are with other types of assessments. Written assessments may not allow them to demonstrate their learning as effectively as oral or presentational activities might.

Because of cultural values, Aboriginal students may be less comfortable and less likely to take part in class discussions or participate assertively in groups. They may more typically be quiet students and reflective learners.

Family and community commitments may also affect Aboriginal students' attendance and their ability to deliver assignments and projects on time, which in turn can affect their ability to demonstrate their learning. Births, marriages, deaths, community and spiritual ceremonies, and other events may result in many days of absence throughout the school year. Responsibilities for younger siblings and other family members may also take students' focus away from schoolwork.

As a result of these circumstances, Aboriginal students may be penalized by a number of common assessment practices, including:
- single rather than multiple assessment methods
- inflexible deadlines (with late penalties or "0" for incomplete assignments)
- time-limited assessments
- marks awarded for class participation and effort
- awarding zeros for incomplete or missing assignments
- failure to match testing to teaching
- surprising students with pop quizzes
- grading first efforts, rather than providing ample time for teaching, practice and feedback before evaluating products (Canady and Hotchkiss 1989).

If a student's absenteeism is adversely affecting that student's learning, discuss this with the student and his or her family. Work together to develop strategies that respect family and cultural values, and support improved attendance.

Fair grading practices

How can teachers ensure that cultural values and life circumstances do not compromise their Aboriginal students' opportunities to demonstrate their learning? Marking and grading practices that are appropriate and culturally aware are an effective place to start.

Many Aboriginal students can successfully meet curriculum requirements, especially when they have opportunities to use multiple assessment methods to demonstrate their learning.

Aboriginal students may struggle with:
- handing assignments in on time
- not having second chances
- being graded on personal and social characteristics, e.g., marks for participation.

Handing assignments in on time

There are many reasons why Aboriginal students may hand in late work. In addition to the cultural and family factors listed earlier, they are, like all adolescents, still learning time-management strategies and how to gauge the amount of work required to complete assignments.

Before using late penalties, teachers need to consider the following.

- Do late penalties produce on-time work in subsequent assignments or do they act as a disincentive for completing the work?

- Do late penalties allow for individual learning needs and personal challenges?

- Do they reflect real-world situations, e.g., does a missed deadline in a work situation result in a similar penalty?

Stiff penalties, such as losing 10 percent per day up to a maximum of 50 percent, distort student achievement and result in a grade that does not reflect what the student has actually learned. Lesser penalties of 1 percent or 2 percent a day up to a lower maximum are more effective in encouraging on-time work while still accurately reflecting student achievement (O'Connor 1999).

Teacher story

> **Meeting students halfway**
> "I accept late assignments. I encourage students to hand in as much as they've been able to complete. I mark the completed sections and the incomplete work separately. I grade the overall assignment and then I also grade the quality of the completed work. That way if a student gets 30% on the incomplete assignment, I can show them that they would have had a 70% or an 80% if they'd completed the work and handed it in on time."

Need for second chances

Aboriginal approaches to education typically provide a student with repeated opportunities to observe, practise and master a skill, much like the apprenticeship model. Reflecting this approach in assignments and tests, teachers can offer students a second-chance assessment, giving them the opportunity to practise their skill and redo the assessment.

Teachers can support Aboriginal students in these circumstances by choosing to emphasize content rather than timing and by allowing students to complete missed tests and assignments.

Evaluating personal and social characteristics

Personal and social characteristics such as effort, participation and attitude are often related to cultural values. Aboriginal students may be quieter and less assertive than many non-Aboriginal students and, as a result, may receive lower grades when these characteristics are factored into an assessment.

In a similar way, motivation and attitude may be difficult to measure—apparent lack of motivation and an inappropriate attitude may reflect more on the cultural or personal relevance of a learning activity than on the personal development of the student.

For an accurate measure of Aboriginal students' learning achievements relative to specific learning outcomes in the programs of study, personal and social characteristics should not be considered as part of the final mark or score of an academic task. It is more appropriate to assess and report on these aspects of learning in other ways, such as through anecdotal comments or as part of students' learning conferences.

Sample strategies for increasing student success on tests and other assessment performance tasks

- Provide an in-class review for major tests to:
  - level the playing field for all students, regardless of how much support they receive at home
  - enable all students to perform better on assessment tasks
  - help students predict what material and tasks will be assessed
  - help students review effectively.

- Help students develop study plans for major assessments to:
  - ensure that assessments are integrated with classroom instruction
  - model learning strategies that students can use across the grades.

- Provide sample questions and practice tasks to:
  - give students opportunities to practise demonstrating their learning within these specific contexts
  - reduce the element of surprise and provide students with the information they need to effectively prepare to demonstrate their knowledge and skills.

- Give students a minimum of three days to prepare for major tests to:
  - give students the time they need to organize material, and review skills and concepts that may have been learned over several months
  - provide the time needed for students to engage in frequent and intense periods of study of 20 to 30 minutes per day (the optimal study schedule identified by research to deepen understanding of new material).

- Audiotape tests or use other assistive technology such as scan-and-read software for less-able readers to create opportunities for all students, whatever their reading level might be, to demonstrate their mastery of skills and concepts. Unless reading abilities are specifically being tested, success should depend on a student's mastery of the specific learner outcomes being tested, not on reading ability.

- Consider the limitations of multiple-choice assessment tasks. They may be easier to score and allow for more consistent scoring from one marker to the next, but developing items that are fair and valid can be challenging and time-consuming. Avoid poorly constructed multiple choice items that fail to measure understanding of a specific skill or concept, or are contrived or misleading. Using only a multiple-choice format on tests may not provide some students with a fair opportunity to show what they know. Students need a range of types of questions to show their learning.

- Be willing to clarify directions during tests because:
  - unless the assessment task is to specifically measure independent reading skills, weak reading skills should not be a barrier to demonstrating learning
  - when more than one student asks for clarification, the directions may be unclear; to be fair, teachers should clarify those directions for the whole class.

- Consider how time-limited tests can affect students' success. Time-limited tests:
  - provide information on how quickly students can process information and develop responses
  - may be appropriate if speed is an important aspect of a skill
  - are not a valid part of a fair testing approach if their sole purpose is to differentiate high-ranking students from lower-ranking ones.

- Help students make themselves comfortable by allowing students to bring an item of significance that allows them to remain calm and focused. For example, they may find comfort in holding a rock given to them by an Elder who has said it will help them find their own strengths.

Effective Assessment Practices

The learning needs and strengths of Aboriginal students can be most effectively supported by assessment practices that:
- offer multiple methods of assessment
- state expectations and timelines clearly
- include elements of self-evaluation.

Multiple assessment

Multiple assessment methods are effective because they:
- create opportunities for Aboriginal students to demonstrate their learning in a variety of ways, such as through presentations, creation of products or written work
- accommodate individual differences, learning preferences and learning strengths
- offer a more complete and multifaceted view of student learning, helping to minimize inconsistencies caused by such factors as discomfort with written assignments or the effect of completing a task on a day when the student was feeling stressed or distracted by personal issues.

Multiple assessment offers students a range of opportunities in a variety of formats in which to demonstrate their learning. These formats can be oral, written, presentational, visual, musical, performance-based—the list is endless. Different types of assessments can measure learning undertaken as a class, independently, in groups and/or in cooperative learning situations.

For example, multiple assessment options for a unit dealing with land claims could include:

- a group project researching and reporting on a local land claims issue
- a work of visual or performance art expressing the spiritual significance of the land to Aboriginal people
- a work of persuasive writing supporting a particular point of view about an historical or current land claim issue
- a short-answer test to review legal, historical and other information about the topic.

Examples of opportunities for multiple assessment include learning tasks such as:

- Venn diagrams
- mathematical word problems
- scripts for radio shows
- reactions to guest speakers, films or videos
- artwork/photographs
- storyboards
- presentations
- raps and poems
- reflective learning logs.

Clear expectations

Assessment practices that are effective support the learning strengths and needs of Aboriginal students by clearly and consistently reflecting learning outcomes. To ensure that assessment practices achieve this, consider the following strategies.

- Integrate assessment into the instructional planning process. This will ensure that assessment progresses naturally out of instruction and relates directly to learning strategies.

- Make sure that assessment is compatible with the instructional approaches used. For example, students learning to proofread and edit work should be assessed on a writing task that demonstrates these skills, not on multiple-choice questions about grammar and language use.

- Include students in the assessment planning process. Let them know why and how assessment information is being gathered.

- Give directions that are clear, complete and appropriate to the ability, age and grade level of the students. Be prepared to repeat and clarify directions.

- Show students examples of work and discuss why the work meets, exceeds or fails to meet expectations.

- Give students opportunities to practise assessment tasks or assignments so that the students become familiar and comfortable with them.

Rubrics as criteria for success

Rubrics are an effective form of assessment to use with Aboriginal students because they clearly and concisely convey assessment expectations. They show the student both the goal of the task and the steps to take in order to reach that goal. To use rubrics effectively with students, consider the following strategies.

- Present a rubric, or construct it in partnership with students prior to beginning the task or assignment.

- Help students examine and analyze samples of work that meet the rubric's various levels of criteria. Discuss how these examples could be improved through revision.

- Rubrics are especially effective in assessing presentations, performances, visual work, and more complex and comprehensive learning activities. When using rubrics for these tasks, it is important to ensure that the assessment criteria move beyond basic knowledge and comprehension, and into higher-order thinking skills that express an understanding of basic knowledge.

For a blackline master of a rubric template, see *Appendix 21: Rubric Template*.

Sample Scoring Rubric for a Venn Diagram

Standard of excellence / outstanding evidence

- ☐ Identifies many ways that two concepts are alike
- ☐ Identifies many ways that concepts are different from one another
- ☐ Uses precise, detailed vocabulary
- ☐ Information contains thought-provoking details
- ☐ Uses subheads to logically sequence and cluster information
- ☐ Clearly and creatively labels all parts of the diagram
- ☐ Has a descriptive and attention-getting title

Well on the way / strong evidence

- ☐ Identifies several ways that two concepts are alike
- ☐ Identifies several ways that concepts are different from one another
- ☐ Uses descriptive vocabulary
- ☐ Information contains interesting details
- ☐ Uses subheads to indicate sequence of information
- ☐ Clearly labels all parts of the diagram
- ☐ Has a descriptive title

Good start / some evidence

- ☐ Identifies some ways that two concepts are alike
- ☐ Identifies some ways that concepts are different from one another
- ☐ Uses appropriate vocabulary
- ☐ Information contains essential details
- ☐ Organizes information
- ☐ Labels main parts of the diagram
- ☐ Has an appropriate title

Just beginning / little evidence

- ☐ Identifies few or incorrect ways that two concepts are alike
- ☐ Identifies few or incorrect ways that concepts are different from one another
- ☐ Uses vague or incorrect vocabulary
- ☐ Information is missing essential details
- ☐ Minimal attempt to organize information
- ☐ Labels on diagram are incomplete
- ☐ Has an incomplete title or is missing a title

Self-evaluation

Student self-evaluation is an especially appropriate form of assessment for Aboriginal students because it encourages independent learning through the awareness and development of inner control and responsibility, both of which reflect strong cultural values.

Teachers may be reluctant to use student self-evaluation because they worry that it does not accurately assess achievement. However, recent studies (Rolheiser and Ross 2000) show that self-evaluation benefits students in a number of ways, including the following.

- Self-evaluation supports cognitive achievement, especially in narrative writing skills. By learning how to evaluate their own work, students become better writers.

- Self-evaluation builds motivation. Students are more likely to take responsibility for their work, to persist through challenges and to gain confidence in their own ability.

- Self-evaluation improves student attitudes towards evaluation. With age, students tend to become cynical about traditional grading methods, but when self-evaluation contributes to final grades, they are more likely to report that the overall evaluation process has been fair and worthwhile.

By creating opportunities for students to reflect on their own performance, self-evaluation provides teachers with information about student effort, persistence, goals, attributions of success and failure, and belief about competence that cannot be gathered any other way.

Self-evaluation, used as one form among multiple assessments, can assist teachers in identifying individual learning needs as well as opportunities for student success.

Some students, parents and teachers may feel that self-evaluation can lead to inflated grades and inaccurate measures of student learning. In fact, when students are taught systematic self-evaluation techniques, their judgement about their own performance becomes increasingly more accurate. When students are partners in establishing the criteria used to judge their work, their understanding of expectations improves, and the gap between their self-evaluation and teacher evaluation narrows (Rolheiser and Ross 2000).

wisdom

Shared

On offering encouragement

"From a traditional perspective, respect for choice is utmost, but healing is a collaborative process. Therefore, offer suggestions without offering directions. There is a difference between encouraging and pushing. And once again, with traditional Native youth, actions will always speak louder than words."

– Garrett et al. 2003, p. 232

Chapter 7

Teaching Aboriginal Students with Learning Disabilities:
Recognizing gifts and strengths

This chapter will help teachers to:
- refine, or perhaps redefine, their understanding of learning disabilities to enable them to see Aboriginal students with learning disabilities as having unique gifts, strengths and needs
- recognize the importance of positive parent involvement in all aspects of the individualized program planning process
- build a repertoire of strategies that will encourage Aboriginal students with learning disabilities to develop the study skills that will help them succeed
- identify and use a wide variety of accommodations to support the success of Aboriginal students with learning disabilities.

Traditional and contemporary Aboriginal cultures are diverse and unique, yet they share the perspective that each individual has the ability to become a fully contributing member of the community. This perspective focuses on the gifts each child possesses and offers a number of frameworks for understanding, guiding, learning from and teaching students with disabilities.

Disabilities as Gifts

Aboriginal worldviews recognize that each student has a unique pattern of learning. Traditionally, each individual was seen as having a gift. The whole community helped individual young people determine how to use their strengths and gifts to serve the community.

The concept of learning disabilities is at odds with the holistic framework of Aboriginal education. Even the term identifies only a part of the child, the part that does not function well as a learner within the education system.

Because of this, it is not uncommon for Aboriginal parents to be reluctant to have their children assessed or labelled as having learning disabilities. Parents may regard psychologists with distrust, wondering if they are working in the best interests of their child. Some Aboriginal families who follow a more traditional way of life may

123

prefer to seek the advice and support of healers or traditional teachers, feeling that psychologists have a limited scope of practice and understanding.

story

Teacher

Disabilities as gifts
"I have come to learn that some students with learning disabilities can successfully process their thoughts through art. Despite first appearances, they often know their topic well. A student who had never successfully written an essay before was struggling to write one about Canadian history. As I was walking around the room, I saw that she was drawing instead of writing. I knew this student liked to draw, so I asked her to create a picture about the topic first. I told her then we'd see if she could write about it. She drew a beautiful picture about British Loyalists coming to Canada. The setting, the people, the action and the reaction—they were all a part of her picture. I suggested that she write a paragraph or two about each part. Then we combined it into an essay. She now knows that by drawing something first, she creates a unique mind map from which to write."

Is It Really a Learning Disability?

Several challenges that students may face in the classroom could appear at first glance to be learning disabilities. These challenges could include sensory or physical disabilities, problems at home, absenteeism, discomfort in school settings, reserved personalities and giftedness.

Sensory or physical disabilities
Learning disabilities are not caused by visual, hearing, speech or mobility impairments. However, if these problems go undiagnosed and without intervention, they will present barriers to learning. Students with these impairments may also have learning disabilities.

Problems at home
Difficult home situations and poverty issues raise many barriers to learning. Students who have not slept or eaten properly may have trouble focusing at school. Many Aboriginal children live in poverty and/or may face multiple incidents of trauma in their lives. For many of these children, daily survival takes priority over daily schoolwork.

Absenteeism

Students may have missed a number of days of school for a variety of reasons. Their commitment to community and to other family members may be stronger than their commitment to their education. Other students may not feel connected or comfortable in school and may develop a pattern of poor attendance. They may be behind in their learning because their exposure to educational concepts has been interrupted. This is different from having a difficulty with learning.

Discomfort in school settings

Some Aboriginal students may not feel safe writing or speaking their thoughts—both public acts in the classroom. They may have been laughed at in the past or they may be worried about appearing unknowing or ignorant, believing they should never make a statement unless they know it to be true. Other students may be unsure of how to ask for help or be uncomfortable asking questions.

Reserved personalities

A quiet student who may seem unresponsive may simply be expressing a cultural comfort with silence. In many traditional cultures, learning to observe is highly valued. Students may need to watch others first before beginning to act themselves.

Giftedness

Students who are very bright may have difficulty organizing their thoughts, focusing on tasks and managing boredom. Their performance in the classroom may not accurately reflect their true potential.

story

Teacher

Time to learn about the printed word
"Many of our students are obviously bright but they start school behind others in terms of literacy skills. It's not so surprising—many of them come from homes where stories, songs and teachings are considered more important than reading a newspaper or a novel. Sometimes teachers will want to test them, thinking that they have a learning disability. I suggest they wait and see—and often these kids adjust. They have strong oral literacy skills. They just need to learn about the printed word."

Identifying Students with Learning Disabilities

When an Aboriginal student is having difficulty learning, a classroom teacher's first step is to use a number of informal methods to assess the student's learning needs, such as talking with the student, observing the student, analyzing the student's work, doing an informal math or reading inventory and/or using screening tests. The teacher can also talk with the parents about their observations and concerns and any out-of-school factors that may be affecting the student's ability to learn. It is important to consider how cultural differences might be affecting the student's performance.

The next step is for the teacher to consult with a school-based team which could include special education teachers, counsellors, Elders, Aboriginal liaison staff, administrators and regular classroom teachers who are knowledgeable about cultural differences, learning difficulties and appropriate strategies. The teacher can try the team's suggestions to see if they make a positive difference in the student's learning.

Formal assessment

If school-based strategies and approaches do not effectively support the student's learning needs, the teacher, in consultation with the parents and with their informed consent, can refer the student for a specialized assessment.

A formal assessment of the student's learning strengths and needs will enable the school to provide the programming the student needs. Aboriginal parents who are wary of assessment need to be reassured that it is an important step in identifying appropriate learning and teaching strategies, and providing the support needed to help their children learn successfully. The Aboriginal liaison worker may be helpful in discussing parents' misgivings and assuring them that the assessment results will be used to create a more effective and responsive educational program for the student.

It is important for teachers to provide Aboriginal parents with detailed information about assessment and to encourage them to discuss any concerns they may have with teachers and other professional staff. Written informed parental consent is required before formal specialized assessment can begin. Informed consent means that parents:
• have a clear understanding of what is involved in the formal assessment of their child
• agree in writing to the carrying out of the formal assessment
• understand that their consent is voluntary and that they may withdraw it at any time.

The language and presentation of consent forms may cause concern among parents. When possible, meet with the parents in person to explain the forms and the purpose of assessment. If the student and parents have built a relationship with an Aboriginal liaison in the school, involve him or her in the process. The role of the liaison is to ensure that parents have the opportunities they need to ask questions, express concerns and gather information.

When talking with parents, use plain language to explain unfamiliar terms. Describe identification and assessment processes. Discuss how there is no single assessment to identify a learning disability. A diagnosis is based on many sources of information, both informal and formal, from the classroom, school staff, consultants, parents and the student. The risks to students in labelling the problem, such as stereotyping, negative self-image or misdiagnosis, must be balanced by the benefits of individualized program planning for them. Labels can direct parents and educators to a body of knowledge that may provide a greater understanding of a student's needs and of beneficial instructional practices. It is important to remember that labels describe typical characteristics, not individual people. Instructional practice must go beyond the label to consideration of the individual's strengths, needs and context of learning.

Once the assessment has been completed, it is important that the teacher and the person who did the assessment meet with the parents and discuss the results of the assessment and the implications for the student's learning. Along with assessment and identification comes the sacred responsibility to see and support the gifts Aboriginal children bring to the classroom. Use the meeting with the parents as an opportunity to begin the collaborative process of describing the child's individual patterns of learning, how their child's learning needs will be addressed in the classroom, and what they, as parents, can do to support their child at home. Parents may need extra time to reflect on this new information and formulate questions. They may benefit from a follow-up meeting at a later date.

From an Aboriginal worldview, it is essential to be nonjudgemental about such things as learning disabilities. All people are accepted, regardless of how they appear to others. This is because a person's spirit is considered to be the most important part of his or her being.

Characteristics of learning disabilities

Learning disabilities are complex and come in many forms and degrees. Often, they may be invisible or misunderstood until they are uncovered by careful observation. Some students may be able to mask their difficulties for a long time by using their strengths or by misbehaving to avoid challenging learning.

Students may come to the classroom with a learning disability already identified. Or a teacher may begin to suspect that a student has a learning disability as the teacher develops a relationship with the student. Observing the student, gathering information from assignments and tests, and talking with the student and the family may help to confirm what the teacher suspects.

Students with learning disabilities are generally described as individuals of at least average intelligence who have difficulties processing information and who experience unexpected difficulties in academic areas. These difficulties cannot be explained on the basis of other disabilities or environmental influences.

Learning disabilities are lifelong. They are not something students outgrow. Students can, however, develop strategies to minimize their impact.

Learning disabilities may be affected by the demands of the environment, so their impact may vary across the lifespan. For example, a student who hears normally but finds that conflicting noise makes it difficult to attend to primary sound may have difficulty in a noisy classroom, but in adult life may function quite well when working in a quiet studio or office space.

Aboriginal students with a learning disability also have learning strengths in one or more areas. The purpose of identifying a student as having a learning disability is to ensure that individualized programming will support their learning needs.

Individual students with learning disabilities will differ in how they learn, the pace at which they learn and the confidence with which they learn. Effective teaching, from elementary through senior high school, requires taking the time to learn about individual students and selecting instructional strategies that best meet each student's special learning needs.

The sooner interventions for learning disabilities are put in place, the more likely students will be to adjust to school and to succeed. Since most students with learning disabilities have difficulty learning to read and write, it is important to pay special attention to early literacy instruction.

Individualized Program Plans (IPPs)

When a student has been identified as having special needs, an Individualized Program Plan (IPP) must be developed.

An IPP is a written commitment of intent, created by a collaborative learning circle that includes the student, teachers and parents, and may also include school administrators and other resource people. The purpose of the IPP is to ensure appropriate planning and instruction for individual students with special needs. An IPP is both a working document and a record of student progress.

An IPP is:
- based on the learning strengths and needs of the student
- created through collaboration
- focused on student success
- an instructional guide for teachers
- a reflective process that encourages students, parents and teachers to continually monitor and assess student progress and program effectiveness
- an accountability tool that helps monitor and evaluate students' programming and progress
- a guide for planning for transition.

Creating a Learning Circle

An IPP for an Aboriginal student is created collaboratively by a Learning Circle whose members sit in the circle as equals. The parents, the student and the classroom teacher form the core of the Learning Circle that supports the student. Elders, Aboriginal liaison staff, resource personnel, teacher assistants and administrators may also be invited to become members of the student's Learning Circle.

Parents and family play a central role in the student's success, beginning with the process of identifying a student's special learning needs and continuing throughout the IPP process.

Parents need, and have a right, to be informed about their child's educational programming and progress. Parents are also valuable sources of information about students and their learning strengths and needs, as well as information about family and cultural contexts. They can provide information and insight that is not available from anyone else.

Parents as partners
Parents are important partners. Start building a positive relationship with parents as soon as the student joins the class. Get to know the parents. Find out where they are from and what their interests and concerns are. Invite them to meet informally at school, or if they prefer, in their home or at a restaurant.

Develop strategies *with* parents, not for parents. Ask parents how they want to be involved and how to best keep them informed about their child's ongoing progress. Encourage them to be actively involved in all stages of creating, implementing and revising the IPP.

Schedule meetings around parents' availability. Ensure that they are kept informed through regular meetings, phone calls and/or informal chats when they come to pick up their child or visit the school for a parent or community event. Communicate in informal ways by:

- talking with parents informally, frequently and regularly
- being positive and proactive.

Draw from the community by using protocol to gather support from the community and to find out what procedures and processes will gain support. Ask Elders, Aboriginal liaisons and/or community leaders to participate in parent meetings and be part of a Learning Circle and the IPP process.

Consider the following strategies for supporting parents throughout the IPP process.

- Help parents understand what an IPP is and the role the process plays in their child's learning. Show them a generic, sample IPP and explain its contents.

- Gather as much information from them as possible about their child's preferences, interests, strengths, experiences, challenges and attitudes. Encourage them to think about their hopes and dreams for their child and share these with the Learning Circle.

- Share information about their role and responsibilities. See *Appendix 22: Parents' Rights and Opportunities to Participate in Educational Decision Making*.

- Help them prepare for IPP conferences. Offer a checklist of questions they might want to consider. Share and explain possible learning strategies and goals.

- Ensure that parents feel welcome at meetings, that they are included in all discussions and that they understand everything that is being discussed.

- Develop the IPP based on input from the Learning Circle, including input from parents.

- Give parents a copy of the IPP to use at home for reference and for writing down observations about their child and any ideas they may have.

- Ensure that parents understand what informed consent is when they are asked to sign IPPs and permissions for specialized assessments. The *Standards for Special Education, Amended June 2004* defines consent as meaning "that parents:
  - have been provided with all information relevant to the activity for which consent is sought
  - understand and agree, in writing, to the carrying out of the activity for which their consent is sought
  - understand that the granting of consent is voluntary and may be withdrawn at any time" (Alberta Learning 2004, p. 4).

Students in the Learning Circle

Build a positive relationship with the students from the first day of class. Observe their approaches to learning, interactions with other students and how they respond to feedback. Talk to them about their learning. Encourage older students to become aware of how they learn.

Building this relationship will help teachers. Gather student input for the IPP about such things as learning preferences and challenges. Encourage them to think about their goals, both short- and long-term.

Include students in the Learning Circle and IPP process. Students who are contributing members of the Learning Circle and actively involved in the IPP process are more likely to take ownership of their learning and become motivated learners.

Teachers and resource personnel in the Learning Circle

Everyone who instructs an Aboriginal student with learning disabilities can be part of the student's Learning Circle and involved in the IPP process. It is especially important to schedule the first few meetings to include as many members of the Learning Circle as possible. If meetings are difficult to schedule, consider meeting informally with other teachers and resource people before or after regular staff meetings to keep them informed of the student's progress and any revisions to the IPP.

The IPP is an ongoing process. Encourage the student's Learning Circle to commit to regular communication, collaboration with outside resources, and ongoing assessment and review of the student's successes and needs.

The IPP Process

The student's Learning Circle participates in all stages of the IPP process, including:

1. ▶ Identifying needs

2. ▶ Setting the direction

3. ▶ Creating a plan

4. ▶ Implementing the plan

5. ▶ Reviewing and revising the plan

6. ▶ Planning for transition.

1. ▶ Identifying needs

Effective IPPs begin with the Learning Circle's understanding of the student. The more the Circle learns about the student's strengths and needs, the more likely they are to create an IPP based on the student's individual learning profile rather than on categorical labels.

Encourage both the student and the parents to provide information about:
- the student's interests, talents and desires
- the student's relevant medical history and health care needs
- the student's hopes and dreams
- what the family can do at home to support the goals of the IPP
- the student's community involvement, after school or caregiver situations that could affect learning.

Consider the student's learning strengths. How can these strengths be used to support learning needs?

Look at the whole student. What are the student's social and behavioural strengths and needs? How could cultural continuity and the classroom community support the student's development?

Essential information
Alberta Education requires that the following essential information be included in the IPP:
- assessment data
- current level of performance and achievement
- identification of strengths and areas of need
- measurable goals and objectives
- procedures for evaluating student progress

- identification of coordinated support services required, including health-related services
- relevant medical information
- required classroom accommodations, such as changes to instructional strategies, assessment procedures, materials, resources, facilities or equipment
- transition plans
- formal review of progress at regularly scheduled reporting periods
- year-end summary
- parent signature, to indicate agreement with the IPP.

2. Setting the direction

In this stage, the Learning Circle reviews all the information it has gathered as well as the resources available. They use this information to develop a list of new skills related to the identified learning needs.

To decide which of the student's learning needs should be the focus of the IPP, the Circle considers each skill and chooses a select few as priorities by exploring questions such as the following.

- How does this skill relate to the student's and parents' hopes and dreams for the future?

- Is this skill age-appropriate?

- Are there opportunities to use this new skill across subjects and settings?

- How will this new skill relate and build on the student's areas of strengths?

- How will the mastery of this skill affect overall learning and achievement?

- Will this skill contribute to the student's independence?

- How long will it take the student to master this skill?

3. Creating a plan

The IPP identifies goals for the student, describing what the student might accomplish in a specific area in one school year. It is important for the plan to describe goals that are realistic and achievable.

To create these goals, consider the following.

- State the goals in plain language.

- Aim to create academic goals around skills that will transfer across content areas.

- Include any appropriate social skill goals that address such needs as attending classes regularly or working independently.

The plan also includes:

- a description of how the student's progress will be reviewed and measured
- a description of which accommodations will be available to support the student's learning needs.

Accommodations, including assistive technology, are described on pages 137–141.

4. Implementing the plan

In this stage of the process:

- teachers put instructional and assessment strategies into practice, making adjustments to short-term goals as needed
- parents and students find ways to support the goals of the IPP at home.

The IPP is a guideline describing a process—it is a working document, subject to change. For successful implementation, consider the following guidelines.

- An IPP is most effective when it is used by everyone responsible for the student's progress.

- Use a variety of assessment strategies to continuously monitor student progress. Attach the assessment information to the IPP. For more information about assessment, see Chapter 6.

- Use the feedback from interim reviews to revise IPP instructional guidelines and student goals.

- Some teachers keep IPPs in binders in their desks where they are accessible for noting observations and revising plans.

- All teachers responsible for the student need to have access to the IPP so they can use it to plan instruction, monitor progress and contribute to evaluating and changing goals and objectives.

5. Reviewing and revising the plan

Review meetings provide an opportunity for the Learning Circle, including the student, to discuss progress. At the year-end review, the Circle reviews the IPP and adds recommendations for the next year.

For a variety of reasons, Aboriginal students may be more likely to change schools during the school year than many non-Aboriginal students. As a result, it is especially important to schedule regular reviews of the IPPs, to ensure that communication with the receiving school is as current as possible and to address transition issues.

To review the effectiveness of a student's IPP, consider the following questions.

- How does the IPP build on the student's individual strengths?
- How does the IPP reflect the student's individual needs?
- How appropriate and effective are the key long- and short-term goals?
- Are the accommodations described currently being used? Are they effective? Do they need to be revised?
- Is the student's participation in the regular curriculum appropriate and successful?
- Does the IPP include provision for multiple-source assessments that effectively address the student's social and behavioural needs and strengths?
- Does the planning for transition reflect cultural concerns and provide a level of support that will help to ensure student success?
- Do all members of the Learning Circle, including the parents and student, have access to the IPP and a way to effectively contribute to assessment and evaluation of the plan?
- What strategies does the IPP use to measure and communicate student progress?
- Is progress monitored frequently? When objectives are met, are new goals set? If the student is not demonstrating progress, does the team review the situation and make changes?

6. Planning for transition

Planning for transition involves:

- identifying the kinds of skills and attitudes that need to be in place for students to be successful in future educational settings
- developing a plan of action to ensure that students acquire these skills and attitudes.

Effective transitions are *planned* with future needs in mind. The planning incorporates an understanding of the learning strengths and needs of the individual student.

Effective transitions are *collaborative* and parents play a key role. As students move through the grades and develop self-advocacy and problem-solving skills, they need to become more involved in planning their transitions.

Effective planning for transition is *comprehensive*. It focuses on social, vocational and interpersonal skills and needs as well as academic skills.

For students with learning disabilities, planning for transition should include specific plans for moving between classrooms, schools and programs as well as from senior high to post-secondary studies or employment.

135

Supporting students through transitions

Whenever possible, arrange face-to-face meetings with the receiving teacher, the student and the parents. This will help ease the transition for everyone. A well-documented, up-to-date IPP will also provide support and direction for the family and the receiving teacher.

story

Teacher

> **Supporting transition to senior high**
> "In our district, when students with learning disabilities are half-way through Grade 9, we arrange for them to take part in activities at the high schools they're interested in—they may join in an art or physical education class, or go on a field trip. We want them to have both social and academic experiences in the new environment. The schools and teachers work together to communicate all the details about the students' IPPs and so on. And we make sure the parents are introduced to the new teachers."

Because some Aboriginal students may move mid-year, there may not always be adequate planning time to help make these transitions more successful. Ongoing work with the student on advocacy and metacognitive skills and strategies is a proactive way to prepare students to communicate effectively with new teachers about their learning strengths and needs.

Financial support for post-secondary education

Help students who are planning a transition to post-secondary settings by making links to Aboriginal student support services in the institutions where they are applying and connecting the students to sources for financial support.

Financial support for post-secondary studies is available to Inuit and Status Indian students living on or off reserve in Canada through the department of Indian and Northern Affairs Canada (INAC). To qualify for this support, students must be identified as Status Indians under the federal *Indian Act*. Most individual First Nations bands establish their own criteria for selection. Students who are Status Indians and on a band list can contact their own band administrative office for more information. Policies and programs vary across the country and across the province. Additional information on specific benefits available is also available from regional and district offices of INAC, Health Canada, First Nations band offices and tribal councils.

The Métis Nation of Alberta provides funding for Métis students entering or returning to post-secondary studies. For more information, contact the Métis Nation of Alberta at 780–423–3237.

In addition, Indian and Northern Affairs Canada provides an online directory, *Scholarships, Bursaries and Awards Guide for Aboriginal Students*, which lists sources of funding available to Aboriginal students entering or returning to post-secondary studies. To access this directory, go to http://sdiprod1.inac.gc.ca/abs/main.asp?lang=E.

See *Appendix 23: Transition Checklist* for a list of types of information that students with special needs should gather to make their transitions to post-secondary studies more successful.

Accommodations and Supports

Some of the challenges faced by students with learning disabilities can be addressed by providing appropriate accommodations. An accommodation is a change or alteration to the regular way a student is expected to learn, complete assignments or participate in the classroom. Accommodations lessen or remove the impact of a student's learning disability, leading to more equal opportunities for success. Accommodations are the school community's way of showing that a student's learning disabilities are accepted and honoured.

Students, teachers and parents sometimes think that accommodations given to students with learning disabilities such as extra time, adaptive devices or special materials, give these students an unfair advantage over other students. In fact, accommodations remove, or at least lessen, the impact of a student's learning disability. As a result, they give the student the same opportunity to succeed as other students.

The three basic types of accommodations are:
- classroom and physical accommodations, e.g., alternative seating, adaptive devices
- instructional accommodations, e.g., providing copies of notes, alternative reading material
- evaluation and testing accommodations, e.g., extra time, oral tests.

To ensure the effective use of accommodations, consider the following strategies.

- Individualize accommodations to match the strengths and needs of individual students.

- Involve students and parents in the process of choosing accommodations. This will increase the likelihood that students will use them.

137

- Select accommodations that are the least intrusive. Avoid using accommodations that isolate students from peers or draw unnecessary attention.

- Specify accommodations in students' IPPs. Only accommodations specified in IPPs and used by students during the course of their regular studies are permitted on provincial achievement tests and diploma examinations.

  For more information on accommodations for provincial achievement tests and diploma examinations, visit www.education.gov.ab.ca/k_12/testing.

- Ensure that students are able to use accommodations consistently. For example, if a student uses a laptop for written work, is there access to an electrical outlet in the student's classrooms? Does the student have access to computers at home?

- Provide time and support for the student to learn how to use an accommodation.

- Monitor the effectiveness of accommodations. Record this information on IPPs so that accommodations will be provided in new settings that students may move to.

Sample accommodations for reading and writing difficulties[15]

- Use less difficult or alternative reading materials within a subject area.
- Reduce the amount of reading required.
- Allow alternative methods of data collection, such as tape recorders, dictation, interviews or graphic organizers.
- Extend time for completing tests and assignments.
- Read directions aloud to students.
- Read test items aloud to students.
- Record directions on audiotapes or CDs.
- Provide written directions for exams ahead of time.
- Use assistive technology, such as books on tape and CD, screen readers, and scan-and-read software.

Sample accommodations for attention difficulties[15]

- Provide alternative seating, e.g., near teacher, facing teacher, at front of class, between students who are good role models, away from distractions.
- Provide personal workspaces, e.g., quiet area for study, extra seat or table, timeout spots, study carrels.
- Permit movement during class activities and testing sessions.

15. From Calgary Learning Centre (Calgary, AB). Used with permission.

- Provide directions in written form.
- Extend time to complete tests and assignments.
- Allow students to complete longer tests in two or three shorter sessions.
- Allow students to take breaks during tests.
- Use place markers, special paper, graph paper or writing templates to encourage students to focus attention.
- Provide visual cues such as arrows and stop signs, on student worksheets.
- Provide quiet, distraction-free areas for completing special assignments and tests.
- Provide earplugs or headphones to screen out distracting sounds.
- Provide checklists for complex assignments.
- Provide specific procedures or processes for turning in completed assignments.

Sample accommodations for memory difficulties[15]

- Provide written outlines.
- Provide directions in written form.
- Provide specific procedures or processes for turning in completed assignments.
- Provide checklists for long, detailed assignments.
- Read standard directions several times at the start of tests.
- Provide visual cues such as arrows and stop signs, on student worksheets.
- Encourage students to refer to references such as personal dictionaries, word lists and arithmetic tables.
- Provide assistive technology for learning, e.g., arithmetic tables, dictionaries, talking calculators, word processors and spell-check devices.

Sample accommodations for fine and gross motor difficulties[15]

- Use assistive and adaptive devices, e.g., slantboards or desktop easels for written work, pencils or pens adapted in size or grip diameter, portable word processors.
- Set realistic and mutually agreed-upon expectations for neatness.
- Reduce or eliminate the need to copy from texts or boards, e.g., provide copies of notes, arrange for students to photocopy peers' notes, provide carbon paper to create duplicate copies of notes.
- Extend time to complete tests and assignments.
- Alter the sizes, shapes or locations of spaces provided for answers.
- Accept keyword responses in place of complete sentences.
- Provide opportunities for students to type answers or answer orally instead of in writing.

Assistive technology for learning

Assistive technology for learning, sometimes called adaptive technology, helps reduce barriers to learning by allowing students with learning disabilities to perform tasks that would otherwise be difficult or impossible for them to do independently. The term refers to items, pieces of equipment or products that are used to help individuals improve their ability to perform specific tasks.

Computers are the most well-known form of assistive technology for learning and there are a variety of computer-related assistive products available, including scan-and-read software, screen readers and voice recognition systems. Not all students with learning disabilities need assistive technology for learning. The decision to try assistive technology for learning should be made on an individual basis, in consultation with the student and parents, after considering the student's strengths, needs and motivation. Some students may benefit from access to technology at both home and school, and may need extra support to do this.

Although assistive technology for learning may be aimed at the needs of a particular student, it is also possible to use assistive technology to benefit a wide range of students. For example, groups of students (with and without special needs) can listen to taped books at a listening centre. This helps create an opportunity for students to participate equally as well as a sense of community and belonging in the classroom.

Examples of Assistive Technology for Learning[16]

	Adaptations	Description
Reading	• Tape-recorded material	• Audio recordings of textbook material and answers to chapter or workbook questions
	• Semantic mapping software	• Software that enables readers to explore and comprehend narrative story or expository writing elements through graphic depictions
	• Electronic word recognition and definition	• Presents definitions of words
	• Screen reader software	• Computerized voice reads material on computer screen
	• Scan-and-read software	• Text is scanned into computer and software computerizes text so it can be read by speech synthesis
Writing	• Pencil grip	• Piece of plastic that is attached where the pencil is grasped
	• Tape recorder	• Standard tape recorder for dictation of written products
	• Semantic mapping software	• Software for outlining and organizing writing
	• Word prediction software	• Software that assists with sentence structure and syntax
	• Speech recognition software	• Voice recognition software that allows student's voice to be converted into written content
	• Electronic spelling devices	• Devices that speak and display, or only display, words and definitions
	• Word processing spell-check option	• Standard spell-check option
	• Speech synthesizer/talking software	• Word processing programs with synthesized voice reading text
Mathematics	• Graph paper	• Centimetre squares for aligning numbers
	• Calculators (including talking calculators and calculators with large keys)	• Devices for checking answers
	• Talking clocks	• Specially designed clocks with synthesized voice that reads time aloud

---

16. Adapted from "Using Assistive Technology Adaptations to Include Students with Learning Disabilities in Cooperative Learning Activities" by D. P. Bryant and B. R. Bryant, 1998, *Journal of Learning Disabilities, 31,* 1, p. 48. Copyright 1998 by PRO-ED, Inc. Adapted with permission.

141

Sample Strategies for Supporting Aboriginal Students with Learning Disabilities

Aboriginal students with learning disabilities may need support in acquiring and practising basic organizational skills, such as time management, note-taking and study skills. They may also need to develop self-advocacy skills.

Time management

Aboriginal students with learning disabilities may have an awareness of time and an understanding of time management that is different from mainstream culture. Time-management skills will help students succeed in time-based classroom processes by developing their ability to decide what is most important for them to do, judge how long it will take, and decide when and how to do it.

Like many students with learning disabilities, Aboriginal students may be disorganized learners. Classroom routines and structures that emphasize organizational strategies will help them succeed and provide them with transferable skills. Consider the following strategies.

- Post a list of materials that students need for class.

- Make sure that expectations, due dates and so on, are explicit and clear, and that they are posted in the classroom.

- Encourage students to write due dates in their daily agendas or homework books.

- Provide students with a model showing how to organize their notebooks. Consider colour-coding notebooks for various subjects. Do periodic notebook checks.

- Schedule weekly or monthly locker and/or desk clean-ups to help students stay organized.

Schedules

Demonstrate how to use daily and weekly schedules. Have students fill in a detailed account of their time for one week to help them develop an awareness of how much of their time they use for daily activities. This will also help them determine their own best times for homework and studying.

Student daily agenda books

Many schools provide students with daily agenda books. They are also widely available at book and office supply stores. Encourage students to use them daily by using the following strategies.

- Set up check systems to ensure that students bring their agenda books to class daily.

- Remind students, when announcing all assignments, tests, due dates and so on, to make note of these in their agendas.

- Have students record all of their out-of-school activities and commitments, including significant FNMI dates, in their agendas.

- Encourage students to use their agendas to plan time for homework and studying.

- Develop positive and creative strategies to help students remember to use and bring their agendas back and forth between home and school. Managing an agenda can be a challenge for those students struggling with organizational skills.

Back planning

Back planning is working backwards from the due date of an assignment or major test to figure out which tasks should be completed by what date in order to meet the deadline.

Students can use a blank calendar page and follow these steps.

- Start with the due date and count the total number of days available to complete the project.

- Break the project down into smaller tasks, and estimate how much time each task will take.

- Work backwards from the due date and record each task in pencil.

- Be prepared to change timelines if something unexpected happens.

- Think of ways to speed up the process for some tasks. For example, get an audio version of a novel if you cannot read it within the deadline.

Back planning calendar for a book report

October

Sunday	Monday	Tuesday	Wednesday	Thursday	Friday	Saturday
			1	2 *Choose book*	3 *Read 20 pages*	4 *Read 20 pages*
5 *Read 20 pages*	6 *Read 20 pages*	7 *Read 20 pages*	8 *Read 20 pages*	9 *Read 20 pages*	10 *Read 20 pages*	11 *Read 20 pages*
12 *Read 20 pages*	13 *Finish book*	14 *Write draft*	15 *Write draft*	16 *Revise draft*	17 *Revise draft*	18 *Expert check*
19 *Expert check*	20 *Final copy*	21	22 *Book report* **DUE**	23	24	25
26	27	28	29	30	31	

Note-taking strategies

Taking notes from class discussion, teacher's lectures or reading a textbook may be a difficult task for many students with learning disabilities.

Effective note taking in class will help students to:

- reinforce and remember what they hear
- become more active listeners
- create a document from which to study.

The following strategies can help students become more effective note takers.

- Introduce students to a variety of different note-taking formats so they can find the one that works best for them.

- Teach the BROIL method.[17] Use the acronym to remind students what kinds of information they need to include in class notes.
  B – on the *B*oard
  R – *R*epeated throughout class, or for many classes
  O – that you say is *O*n the test
  I – that they think is *I*mportant
  L – in a *L*ist.

- When giving a lecture, provide students with organizers outlining key points so they can fill in the details. Examples include web organizer, linear topic list, main points in one column with room for details or cloze-style sentences.

17. From Foothills Academy (Calgary, Alberta). Used with permission.

- If students are copying notes from the board or overhead, encourage them to personalize the information by creating related mind maps, charts or questions and answers.

For more ideas about note taking, see *Teaching Students with Learning Disabilities* (Alberta Education, 1996), Book 6 of the *Programming for Students with Special Needs* series, pp. 117–121, 196–197 and *Make School Work for You* (Alberta Learning, 2001), pp. 30–34.

Study skills

Aboriginal students with learning disabilities may have a good knowledge of the material but may not have effective study skills. Consider the following suggestions for helping students do better on tests.

- Give students plenty of advance notice about upcoming tests; aim for at least one week. Complete a study guide with students so they have clear guidelines for test content and format.

- Encourage students to use their time-management skills to create a study schedule, by back planning study tasks up to the day of the test.

- Teach students strategies for studying for tests, including:
  - highlighting keywords
  - creating webs for individual topics
  - using flash cards
  - making up questions
  - making up *Jeopardy*-style questions
  - reviewing activity sheets and class notes
  - making up cloze statements
  - practising drawings from the unit
  - teaching someone else the information
  - making up a practice test.

For more ideas about study and test-taking skills, see *Make School Work for You* (Alberta Learning, 2001), pp. 35–48.

Decision-making and Problem-solving Strategies

Learning and practising decision-making and problem-solving strategies will help Aboriginal students with learning disabilities begin to take charge of their own success in the classroom and beyond. Decision making can be a linear, logical process—and it can also be an intuitive process, based on what "feels right." Both approaches are valid. Offer students opportunities to make decisions using both of the approaches below.

145

When working with students on decision-making skills, remind them that there is often not a single "right" decision—every choice has up sides and down sides. Some decisions may evolve over time—students will often have opportunities to re-examine their choices and change their minds.

Step-by-step decision making

- *Define the decision.* For example, "Since I only have time for one extracurricular activity this term, what should it be?"

- *Decide what the choices are.* For example, "I could fit basketball or jazz band into my schedule. Which should I choose?"

- *Gather information.* For example, find out when practices and rehearsals are scheduled, when games and performances happen, skill levels required for each activity, time commitment required for each, whether friends are taking part, and any other relevant information.

- *Process the information.* For example, make a "Plus and Minus" list for both alternatives.

- *Choose the option.* Identify which choice has the most positives and fewest negatives.

See *Appendix 24: Decision-making Tree* for a graphic organizer to help students organize and record information for decision making.

"Feels right" decision making

This approach helps students tune into their intuition—their gut feelings about a decision. It just "feels right."

- Encourage students to take time with this process. Intuition cannot be rushed.

- Have them research the decision and find out all they can about the options.

- Suggest they try the step-by-step decision-making process and then pay attention to how they feel about the "logical" choice.

- Encourage them to stay open and use the process to discover how they feel.

- Suggest they go through each option, imagining as clearly as they can how they would feel actually taking that option.

- Encourage students to "sleep on it!"

For a blackline master to support the decision-making process, see *Appendix 24: Decision-making Tree.*

Influences on decision-making circle

Students need to understand what factors influence their decision making. Use a graphic organizer such as Appendix 25 to help students become more aware of how they make decisions, and where they can get additional advice and support to make good decisions.

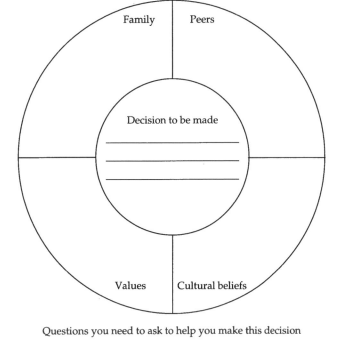

Questions you need to ask to help you make this decision

Adapted from Alberta Learning, *Kindergarten to Grade 9 Health and Life Skills Guide to Implementation* (Edmonton, AB: Alberta Learning, 2002), p. C.39.

For a blackline master to support identifying influences, see *Appendix 25: Influences on Decision Making.*

Students and self-advocacy

For many Aboriginal students, the ability to self-advocate is an important factor to their success at school. Self-advocacy means speaking out and taking positive action to make your situation better. Students learn to self-advocate from observing their teachers and parents advocate on their behalf. They develop self-advocacy skills through modelling, role-play, practice and evaluation.

- Maintain an ongoing dialogue with students about their learning strengths and needs. Encourage them to help plan their program, make decisions, set goals and reflect on their progress.

147

- Encourage students to monitor their own progress through self-assessment. Help them recognize and talk about their learning strengths and needs.

- Self-advocates need to be informed and organized. Model strategies for these skills and encourage students to use them.

- An important part of self-advocacy is the ability to positively influence others. Encourage students to show their appreciation to others who contribute to their learning and success at school.

- Recognize how challenging self-advocacy may be for Aboriginal students and support their efforts.

Other Alberta Education Resources

For more information and sample strategies for supporting students with learning disabilities, see the following Alberta Education resources:

- *Teaching Students with Learning Disabilities* (1996), Book 6 of the *Programming for Students with Special Needs* series

- *Unlocking Potential: Key Components of Programming for Students with Learning Disabilities* (2003)*

- *The Parent Advantage: Helping Children Become More Successful Learners at Home and School, Grades 1–9* (1998)

- *Make School Work for You: A Resource for Junior and Senior High Students Who Want to be More Successful Learners* (2001)

- *A Handbook for Aboriginal Parents of Children with Special Needs* (2000)* and accompanying video *Our Treasured Children* (2000)

- *The Learning Team: A Handbook for Parents of Children with Special Needs* (2003)*

- *Individualized Program Planning* (2005)

- *Building on Success: Helping Students Make Transitions from Year to Year* (2005).

There are also a number of other Alberta Education resources to help teachers program for students with special needs:

- *Teaching Students who are Gifted and Talented* (2000), Book 7 of the *Programming for Students with Special Needs* series

- *Teaching Students with Emotional Disorders and/or Mental Illnesses* (2000), Book 8 of the *Programming for Students with Special Needs* series

- *Teaching Students with Autism Spectrum Disorders* (2003)*, Book 9 of the *Programming for Students with Special Needs* series

- *Teaching Students with Fetal Alcohol Spectrum Disorder: Building Strengths, Creating Hope* (2004)*, Book 10 of the *Programming for Students with Special Needs* series

- *The Journey: A Handbook for Parents of Children who are Gifted and Talented* (2004)*.

Resource titles marked with an asterisk (*) can be downloaded free-of-charge from the Alberta Education Web site at www.education.gov.ab.ca/k_12/specialneeds/.

Print copies of all of the resources listed on pages 148–149 can be purchased from the Learning Resources Centre. Order online at www.lrc.education.gov.ab.ca/ or telephone 780–427–2767.

Glossary of Terms

This glossary is adapted from the Aboriginal Studies 10–20–30 program of studies. The terms and definitions, while not prescriptive, take into consideration Aboriginal diversity and also relate to the overall generic understandings of Aboriginal historical chronology. The terms and definitions have been obtained from the following sources:

Aboriginal Policy Framework (APF)
Government of Alberta. *Strengthening Relationships: The Government of Alberta's Aboriginal Policy Framework.* Edmonton, AB: Government of Alberta, 2000.

Aboriginal Affairs and Northern Development (AAND)
Aboriginal Affairs and Northern Development. "Terms and Definitions." June 1, 2001. http://www.aand.gov.ab.ca/PDFs/terms_definitions.pdf (Accessed July 2005).

Indian and Northern Affairs Canada (INAC)
Indian and Northern Affairs Canada. "Terminology." July 2003. http://www.ainc-inac.gc.ca/pr/info/tln_e.html (Accessed July 2005).

Knots in a String (Knots)
From *Knots in a String: An Introduction to Native Studies in Canada* by Peggy Brizinski. Copyright 1993 University Extension Press. Reprinted by permission of University Extension Press, University of Saskatchewan.

Western Canadian Protocol for Collaboration in Basic Education (WCP)
Western Canadian Protocol for Collaboration in Basic Education. *The Common Curriculum Framework for Aboriginal Language and Culture Programs: Kindergarten to Grade 12.* [N.p.] Western Canadian Protocol for Collaboration in Basic Education, 2000.

Aboriginal Peoples
The descendants of the original inhabitants of North America. The Canadian Constitution [*Constitution Act, 1982*, s. 35] recognizes three groups of Aboriginal people—Indians, Métis people and Inuit. These are three separate peoples with unique heritages, languages, cultural practices and spiritual beliefs. (INAC)

Aboriginal Rights

Rights that some Aboriginal peoples of Canada hold as a result of their ancestors' longstanding use and occupancy of the land. The rights of certain Aboriginal peoples to hunt, trap and fish on ancestral lands are examples of Aboriginal rights. Aboriginal rights will vary from group to group depending on the customs, practices and traditions that have formed part of their distinctive cultures. (INAC)

Band

A body of Indians for whose collective use and benefit lands have been set apart or money is held by the Crown, or declared to be a band for the purposes of the *Indian Act*. Each band has its own governing band council, usually consisting of one chief and several councillors. Community members choose the chief and councillors by election, or sometimes through traditional custom. The members of a band generally share common values, traditions and practices rooted in their ancestral heritage. Today, many bands prefer to be known as First Nations. (INAC)

A Band is defined in the *Indian Act* as a body of Indians for whose common use and benefit lands have been set aside or monies held by the Government of Canada or declared by the Governor in Council to be a Band. Most Bands prefer to be referred to as First Nations. (AAND)

Band Membership

What an individual Indian has when he or she is a recognized member of a Band and whose name appears on an approved Band List. Where a Band has adopted its own membership code, it may define who has a right to membership in the Band, so being a Status Indian is not necessarily synonymous with being a Band member. Status Indians who are not band members are listed in the General List. (AAND)

Bill C–31

The pre-legislation name of the 1985 *Act to Amend the Indian Act*. This act eliminated certain discriminatory provisions of the *Indian Act*, including the section that resulted in Indian women losing their Indian status when they married non-Status men. Bill C–31 enabled people affected by the discriminatory provisions of the old *Indian Act* to apply to have their Indian status and membership restored. (INAC)

This is an *Act to Amend the Indian Act*. It was enacted in June 1985. This legislation amended the *Indian Act* to remove discriminatory clauses against women, restore status and membership rights, and increase Indian control over their own affairs. Those people who have been reinstated as Status Indians under this *Act*, are often referred to as Bill C–31 Indians. (AAND)

Culture

The collection of rules, values and attitudes held by a society which allows people to communicate, to interpret behaviour, and to attach shared meaning to behaviour and events (Knots, p. 372).

The customs, history, values and languages that make up the heritage of a person or people and contribute to that person's or people's identity. (WCP)

First Nations

Usually used to refer to a politically autonomous band under the *Indian Act*—a nation of First Peoples.

The term First Nations is preferred by many Aboriginal peoples and is used to refer to the various governments of the first peoples of Canada. The term First Nations is preferred over the terms Indians, Tribes and Bands, which are used extensively by the federal, provincial and territorial governments. (WCP)

A term that came into common usage in the 1970s to replace the word "Indian," which some people found offensive. Although the term First Nation is widely used, no legal definition of it exists. Among its uses, the term "First Nations peoples" refers to the Indian peoples in Canada, both Status and Non-Status. Some Indian peoples have also adopted the term "First Nation" to replace the word "band" in the name of their community. (INAC)

The people of the First Nations are the descendants of the original inhabitants of North America. … Some 117,465 persons in Alberta identified themselves as North American Indian during the 1996 Canada Census. A registered Indian is a person registered under the *Indian Act*. (APF)

Indian

A term with many usages: could be a person of Indian ancestry, a Status Indian under the *Indian Act*, or a Treaty Indian.

Indian peoples are one of three groups of people recognized as Aboriginal in the *Constitution Act*, 1982. It specifies that Aboriginal people in Canada consist of Indians, Inuit and Métis. Indians in Canada are often referred to as: Status Indians, non-Status Indians and Treaty Indians. (INAC)

Indian Act

Canadian legislation first passed in 1876 and amended many times since then; defines an Indian in relation to federal obligation and sets out a series of regulations applying to Indians living on reserves.

Canadian federal legislation, first passed in 1876, and amended several times since. It sets out certain federal government obligations and regulates the management of Indian reserve lands, Indian moneys and other resources. Among its many provisions, the *Indian Act* currently requires the Minister of Indian Affairs and Northern Development to manage certain moneys belonging to First Nations and Indian lands, and to approve or disallow First Nations by-laws. (INAC)

Indigenous People

Refers to all inhabitants originating in or native to a particular country, and their descendants.

Inuit

An Aboriginal people in northern Canada, who live in Nunavut, Northwest Territories, Northern Quebec and Northern Labrador. The word means "people" in the Inuit language—Inuktitut. The singular of Inuit is Inuk. (INAC)

Métis

People of mixed First Nation and European ancestry who identify themselves as Métis people, as distinct from First Nations people, Inuit or non-Aboriginal people. The Métis have a unique culture that draws on their diverse ancestral origins, such as Scottish, French, Ojibway and Cree. (INAC)

A term for people of mixed Aboriginal and European ancestry. The history of the Métis dates back to the days of the fur trade when Aboriginal people, particularly the Cree, and French or French-Canadian people married. Although the Métis have historically been refused political recognition by the federal government, they were recognized as Aboriginal people in the *Constitution Act* of 1982. The Métis are excluded from registration in the *Indian Act*. They were allotted money scrip or land scrip. (WCP)

A French word meaning "mixed blood" which usually refers to people of mixed ancestry who emerged during the days of the fur trade when Europeans and Indian people had children. The Métis are recognized as Aboriginal people in the *Constitution Act*, 1982. (AAND)

Métis Settlements
Métis Settlements Accord 1989 (APF)
In 1989 the Government of Alberta and the Federation of Métis Settlement Associations signed an historic accord. This led to the cooperative development of unique legislation that establishes the only land base and the only form of legislated Métis government in Canada. Proclaimed in 1990, the legislation includes: the *Métis Settlements Act*, the *Métis Settlements Land Protection Act*, the *Constitution of Alberta Amendment Act* and the *Métis Settlements Accord Implementation Act*.

Under the *Métis Settlements Act*, Métis means a person of Aboriginal ancestry who identifies with Métis history and culture.

The legislation established eight Settlement Corporations (Buffalo Lake, East Prairie, Elizabeth, Fishing Lake, Gift Lake, Kikino, Paddle Prairie and Peavine), the Métis Settlements General Council, the Métis Settlements Transition Commission and the Métis Settlements Appeal Tribunal.

An elected Settlement Council governs each Métis Settlement. The members of the Settlement Councils comprise the Métis Settlements General Council, which elects a four-person executive. The General Council deals with matters that affect the collective interests of the eight Settlements and holds the Letters Patent for the Settlement lands.

Nation
A group of native people with common ancestry who are socially, culturally, politically and linguistically united (Knots, p. 374).

Non-Status Indian
A term that is frequently used and which usually means a person who is not registered as an Indian. Often Indian people lost their right to be registered as an Indian as it is defined by the *Indian Act*. For example, prior to 1985, women who married non-Indian men lost their status. The enactment of Bill C–31 in 1985, has restored Indian status to those who lost it through marriage. (AAND)

An Indian person who is not registered as an Indian under the *Indian Act*. (INAC)

Reserve
Tract of land, the legal title to which is held by the Crown, set apart for the use and benefit of an Indian band. (INAC)

The *Indian Act* describes a reserve as lands which have been set apart for the use and benefit of a Band, and for which the legal title rests with the Crown in right of Canada. The federal government has primary jurisdiction over these lands and the people living on them. (AAND)

Status Indian
A person who is registered as an Indian under the *Indian Act*. The act sets out the requirements for determining who is an Indian for the purposes of the *Indian Act*. (INAC)

A person who has been registered or is entitled to be registered according to the *Indian Act*. Most Registered Indians are members of an Indian Band. By virtue of the *Indian Act*, the Department of Indian Affairs and Northern Development is responsible for providing support and services to all Registered Indians. (AAND)

An Indian person who is registered as an Indian under the *Indian Act* and thus recognized by the federal government as an Indian and accorded the accompanying rights, benefits and restrictions of the *Indian Act* and related policies (Knots, p. 376).

Treaty Indian
A person affiliated with a First Nation that has signed, or whose ancestors signed, a Treaty and who now receives land rights and entitlements as prescribed in a Treaty. Not all First Nations have signed treaties; for example, in British Columbia there are almost no treaties. (AAND)

A Status Indian who belongs to a First Nation that signed a treaty with the Crown. (INAC)

Treaty Rights
First Nations signed treaties with various British colonial and, later, Canadian governments before and after Confederation in 1867. No two treaties are identical, but they usually provide for certain rights, including reserve lands, annuities (a small sum of money paid each year), and hunting and fishing rights. The treaty rights of an individual Treaty Indian will depend on the precise terms and conditions of the treaty that his or her First Nation signed.

Special rights to lands and entitlements that Indian people legally have as a result of treaties. (AAND)

Worldview
The worldview of the Aboriginal cultures is distinct from the worldview of the mainstream culture in Canada. This worldview presents human beings as inhabiting a universe made by the Creator and striving to live in respectful relationship with nature, one another and oneself. Each Aboriginal culture expresses this worldview in different ways, with different practices, stories and cultural products. (WCP)

Appendices

1. Treaty Area Map of Alberta
2. First Nations and First Nations Communities in Alberta
3. Métis Settlements and Regional Zones in Alberta
4. First Nations and Métis Language Groups in Alberta
5. Guidelines for Talking Circles
6. Evaluating Resources About Aboriginal Peoples
7. Aboriginal Parents Offer Advice to Other Parents
8. Aboriginal Organizations and Agencies
9. Fishbone
10. T-chart
11. Venn Diagram
12. P–M–I Chart
13. Place Mat
14. K–W–L Chart
15. Brainstorm
16. Three-step Interview
17. Independent Study Planner
18. Choosing a Service Learning Project
19. Making It Happen
20. Reflecting on Our Service Learning
21. Rubric Template
22. Parents' Rights and Opportunities to Participate in Educational Decision Making
23. Transition Checklist
24. Decision-making Tree
25. Influences on Decision Making

Treaty Area Map of Alberta

http://www.aand.gov.ab.ca/PDFs/reserves_map.pdf

© 1998 Government of Alberta

First Nations and First Nations Communities in Alberta

First Nations

Treaty 6
Alexander
Alexis
Beaver Lake
Cold Lake
Enoch
Ermineskin
Frog Lake
Kehewin
Louis Bull
Montana
O'Chiese
Paul
Saddle Lake
Samson Cree
Stoney
Sunchild Cree

Treaty 7
Blood Tribe
Piikani
Siksika
Stoney (Nakoda)
Tsuu T'ina Nation

Treaty 8
Alexis
Athabasca Chipewyan
Beaver
Bigstone Cree
Chipewyan Prairie
Dene Tha'
Driftpile River
Duncan's
Fort McKay
Fort McMurray
Heart Lake
Horse Lake
Kapawe'no
Little Red River
Loon River Cree
Lubicon Lake
Mikisew Cree
Sawridge
Sturgeon Lake
Sucker Creek
Swan River
Tallcree
Whitefish Lake
Woodland Cree

- A **band** is a term defined by the *Indian Act* to describe a territorially-based group of First Nations people who share a common culture and ancestry.
- Today, many bands prefer to be known as First Nations.
- A First Nation (or band) has its own governing band council, usually consisting of one chief and several councillors.
- A First Nation (or band) may have more than one First Nation community (or reserve).

First Nations and First Nations Communities in Alberta (continued)

Communities

Treaty 6
Alexander
Alexis
Beaver Lake
Blue Quills First
  Nation Reserve
Buck Lake
Cardinal River
Cold Lake
Elk River
Ermineskin
Kehewin
Louis Bull
Makaoo
Montana
O'Chiese
O'Chiese Cemetery
Pigeon Lake
Puskiakiwenin
Saddle Lake
Stony Plain
Sunchild Cree
Unipouheos
Wabamun
Whitefish Lake

Treaty 7
Bearspaw
Big Horn
Blood
Piikani
Piikani (timber limit)

Siksika
Tsuu T'ina
Wesley Chiniki

Treaty 8
Allison Bay
Amber River
Assineau River
Beaver Ranch
Bistcho Lake
Boyer River
Bushe River
Calling Lake
Carcajou Settlement
Charles Lake
Child Lake
Chipewyan
Clear Hills
Clearwater
Coin Lake
Cornwall Lake
Cowper Lake
Devil's Gate
Dog Head
Driftpile River
Duncan's
Fort McKay
Fort Vermilion
Fox Lake
Freeman
Gregoire Lake
Grouard

Halcro
Hay Lake
Heart Lake
Horse Lake
House Rover Indian
  Cemetery
Jackfish Point
Janvier
Jean Baptiste Gambler
John D'Or Prairie
Namur Lake
Namur River
Old Fort
Pakashan
Peace Point
Sand Point
Samson
Sawridge
Sturgeon Lake
Sucker Creek
Swan River
Tallcree
Trout Lake
Upper Hay River
Utikoomak Lake
Wabasca
Wadlin Lake
Whitecourt
William McKenzie
Winefred Lake
Woodland Cree
Zama Lake

- A **reserve** is land set aside, or reserved, by the federal government for the use and benefit of a First Nation. The Crown holds the legal title to reserve lands and the federal government has jurisdiction over reserves and the people living there.
- Many First Nations now prefer the term "First Nation community" and no longer use the term "reserve."
- A First Nation community (or reserve) can also be home to two or more First Nations (or bands).

Métis Settlements and Regional Zones in Alberta

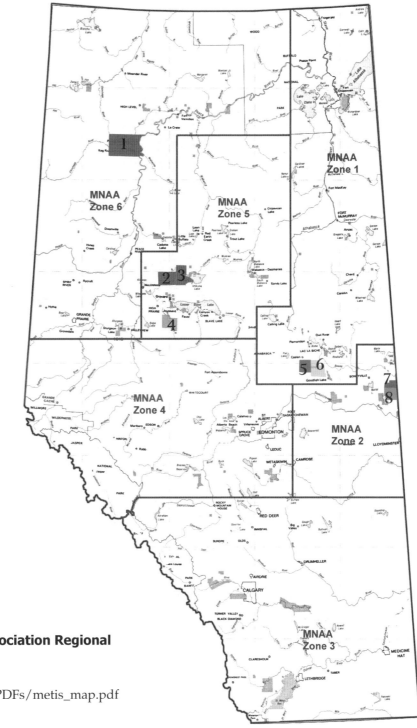

Métis Settlements

1. Paddle Prairie
2. Peavine
3. Gift Lake
4. East Prairie
5. Buffalo Lake
6. Kikino
7. Elizabeth
8. Fishing Lake

Métis Nation of Alberta Association Regional Zones

http://www.aand.gov.ab.ca/PDFs/metis_map.pdf

© 1998 Government of Alberta

Appendix 4

First Nations and Métis Language Groups in Alberta

One way to be more respectful of the diversity that characterizes Aboriginal groups is to learn and use appropriate Aboriginal names to refer to various language groups.

- Blackfoot (Siksika, Kainai, Piikani) – concentrated in southern Alberta

- Dene Soultine (Chipewyan) – concentrated in northern Alberta

- Dene tha (Slavey) – concentrated in northern Alberta

- Dunne´za (Beaver) – concentrated in northern Alberta

- Métis Cree – concentrated in north central Alberta

- Michif (French) – concentrated in central northeastern Alberta

- Stoney (Nakoda Sioux) – concentrated in west central Alberta

- Plains Cree – concentrated in central and southern Alberta

- Saulteaux – concentrated in western Alberta

- Tsuu T´ina – concentrated in south central Alberta

- Woodland Cree – concentrated in northern Alberta

Guidelines for Talking Circles

Talking circles are based on the sacred tradition of sharing circles. People leading a traditional sharing circle will have a blessing from an Elder to do this, and will use special prayers and sacred objects in the ceremony.

The purpose of the less formal talking circle, used as part of classroom instruction, is to create a safe environment in which students can share their point of view with others. In a Talking Circle, each one is equal and each one belongs. Participants in a Talking Circle learn to listen and respect the views of others. The intention is to open hearts to understand and connect with one another.

- Participants sit in a circle. The circle symbolizes completeness.

- Review ground rules with participants. For example:
    - Everyone's contribution is equally important.
    - State what you feel or believe starting with "I-statements," e.g., "I feel …"
    - All comments are addressed directly to the question or the issue, not to comments another person has made. Both negative and positive comments about what anyone else has to say should be avoided.

- An everyday object such as a rock or pencil is sometimes used as a talking object.

- When the talking object is placed in someone's hands, it is that person's turn to share his or her thoughts, without interruption. The object is then passed to the next person in a clockwise direction.

- Whoever is holding the object has the right to speak and others have the responsibility to listen.

- Everyone else is listening in a nonjudgemental way to what the speaker is saying.

- Silence is an acceptable response. There must be no negative reactions to the phrase, "I pass."

- Speakers should feel free to express themselves in any way that is comfortable; by sharing a story, a personal experience, by using examples or metaphors, and so on.

Evaluating Resources About Aboriginal Peoples

Students should be presented with accurate, objective information about Aboriginal cultures, contributions and experiences over time. Use the following types of sample questions when evaluating a potential resource to help decide whether a resource is appropriate or not.

Aboriginal Resource Checklist

1. Is the resource recognized by the Aboriginal community?

Yes	No	N/A	Has the resource been validated by Aboriginal groups and/or Elders?
Yes	No	N/A	Has the resource been validated by Aboriginal authors and/or scholars?
Yes	No	N/A	Is the author qualified to deal with Aboriginal content?
Yes	No	N/A	Has the resource been approved for use in other settings?

Comments: _____

_____

_____

2. Is the resource culturally authentic?

Yes	No	N/A	Is the Aboriginal worldview accurately portrayed and/or interpreted?
Yes	No	N/A	Are Aboriginal values and beliefs accurately portrayed and/or interpreted?
Yes	No	N/A	Are Aboriginal traditions and customs accurately portrayed and/or interpreted?
Yes	No	N/A	Are cultural and societal roles accurately portrayed?
Yes	No	N/A	Is cultural diversity within the Aboriginal group recognized?
Yes	No	N/A	Is the way of life of Aboriginals in both the present and the past accurately portrayed?

Comments: _____

_____

_____

Evaluating Resources About Aboriginal Peoples
(continued)

3. Is the resource historically accurate?

   Yes   No   N/A   Are significant events of the past accurately portrayed?

   Yes   No   N/A   Is the process surrounding decisions, documents (treaties, etc.) accurately portrayed?

   Yes   No   N/A   Are Aboriginal contributions over time accurately portrayed?

Yes   No   N/A   Has past contact with other cultures been accurately portrayed?

Yes   No   N/A   Are historical events accurately linked with life today?

Yes   No   N/A   Are dates and time periods accurate?

Comments: _____

_____

_____

4. Is the resource balanced and objective?

Yes   No   N/A   Is the resource free of stereotypical descriptions that present any person, group or culture in a less than objective manner?

Yes   No   N/A   Does the resource refer to any person, group or culture in a solely positive or negative manner?

Yes   No   N/A   Is there evidence of any bias for or against a particular person, group or culture?

Yes   No   N/A   Are multiple points of view and/or interpretations included and given equal weight?

Comments: _____

_____

_____

5. Are the language and terminology accurate and respectful?

Yes   No   N/A   Are all people, groups and cultures referred to or named respectfully or in a way that will not cause offence?

Yes   No   N/A   Is the resource free of all derogatory terms for any culture or group?

Comments: _____

_____

_____

Evaluating Resources About Aboriginal Peoples
(continued)

6. Are the graphics culturally accurate and/or respectful?

Yes   No   N/A   Are traditional structures, items of clothing and situations accurately portrayed?

Yes   No   N/A   Are people shown in attire that is appropriate for the situation portrayed?

Yes   No   N/A   Are the graphics free of sacred items that should not be displayed for all to see?

Comments: _____

_____

_____

7. Is the resource based on information from recognized sources?

Yes   No   N/A   Is/are the author(s) recognized as (a) qualified, objective source(s) of information about all of the cultures, situations and/or events covered in the resource?

Yes   No   N/A   Is there evidence that other contributors to the resource were carefully and objectively chosen?

Yes   No   N/A   Are all contributors recognized as qualified, objective sources of topically relevant information?

Comments: _____

_____

_____

After you have answered all the questions, look back at the items you have marked "No." Do they raise some concerns or problems with the resource?

If so, discuss the resource with colleagues or people from your local Aboriginal community and decide whether all or parts of the resource can be used in class.

Be aware that it is acceptable to use a resource to illustrate a point of view or opinion, as long as you use another resource that illustrates an opposing or alternative point of view.

Aboriginal Parents Offer Advice to Other Parents

- Come to the school—the school belongs to your child. Visit your child's school anytime throughout the school year. At the beginning of the year, ask your child's teacher how to make arrangements to visit the classroom.

- Let your voice be heard by the teacher and, if need be, by the administration. If you have a concern, continue to speak up, as it is the only way positive changes will happen.

- Ask to sit in on classes to see what is happening.

- Talk with other parents who have children in the class.

- Look for local parent support groups and find out about other resources.

- Get to know the teacher by name and make sure he or she knows how to contact you.

- Tell the teacher how you may be contacted if you don't have a phone.

- Make an appointment with the teacher to discuss any specific concerns. Make arrangements to telephone or write a letter if you are unable to meet.

- Ask that the teacher, principal, liaison worker or school counsellor meet with you in your home if you would feel more comfortable meeting there.

- Read the school newsletters, as they often contain valuable information that concerns your child.

- Become familiar with the school's policies and procedures about attendance, discipline and other issues.

- Don't be afraid to ask questions.

- Go to all parent-teacher conferences.

- Keep all school information in one place so it's handy for meetings at the school or when seeing others in the community about your child.

- Volunteer to share a craft or special skill from your culture.

Adapted from Alberta Learning, *A Handbook for Aboriginal Parents of Children with Special Needs* (Edmonton, AB: Alberta Learning, 2000), pp. 30–31.

Aboriginal Organizations and Agencies

Treaty 8 Education

Treaty 8 Education Coordinator
Treaty 8 First Nation of Alberta
Santa Fe Plaza
18178 – 102 Avenue
Edmonton, AB T5S 1S7
Telephone: 780–444–9366
Fax: 780–444–9369
E-mail: shelleyw@treaty8.org
Web site: www.treaty8.org

Athabasca Tribal Council
Director of Education
9206 McCormick Drive
Fort McMurray, AB T9H 1C7
Telephone: 780–791–6538
Fax: 780–791–0946

Kee Tas Kee Now Tribal Council
Director of Education
Box 120
Atikameg, AB T0G 0C0
Telephone: 780–767–2116
Fax: 780–767–2447

Lesser Slave Lake Indian Regional Council
Director of Education
Box 269
Slave Lake, AB T0G 2A0
Telephone: 780–849–4943
Fax: 780–849–4975

North Peace Tribal Council
Director of Education
Box 1889
High Level, AB T0H 1Z0
Telephone: 780–926–3446
Fax: 780–926–4075

Western Cree Tribal Council
Director of Education
Box 2129
Valleyview, AB T0H 3N0
Telephone: 780–524–5978
Fax: 780–524–2898

Treaty 7 Education Authorities

Kainai Board of Education
Box 240
Stand Off, AB T0L 1Y0
Telephone: 403–737–3966
Fax: 403–737–2361

Peigan Band
Box 130
Brocket, AB T0K 0H0
Telephone: 403–965–3910
Fax: 403–965–3713

Siksika Board of Education
Box 1099
Siksika, AB T0J 3W0
Telephone: 403–734–5220
Fax: 403–734–2505

Stoney Tribal Administration
Box 238
Morley, AB T0L 1N0
Telephone: 403–881–3591
Fax: 403–881–3860

Tsuu T'ina Nation
205, 9911 Chula Boulevard S.W.
Tsuu T'ina Sarcee, AB T2K 3J6
Telephone: 403–238–6112
Fax: 403–974–1449

Aboriginal Organizations and Agencies (continued)

Treaty 6 Education

Treaty Six Education
Suite #202, 17510 – 107 Avenue
Edmonton, AB T5S 1E9
E-mail: mail@treatysixeducation.org
Toll free: 1–877–430–4200
Web site: treatysixeducation.org

Alexander First Nation
Box 3449
Morinville, AB T8R 1S3
Telephone: 780–939–3551
Fax: 780–939–3523

Alexis Nakota Sioux Nation
Box 135
Glenevis, AB T0E 0X0
Telephone: 780–967–4878
Fax: 780–967–4999

Beaver Lake Cree Nation
Amisk Community School
Bag 5000
Lac La Biche, AB T0A 2C0
Telephone: 780–623–4548
Fax: 780–623–4659

Cold Lake First Nation
Box 1769
Cold Lake, AB T9M 1P4
Telephone: 780–594–7183
Fax: 780–594–3577

Enoch Cree Nation
Box 90
Enoch, AB T7X 3Y3
Telephone: 780–418–4270
Fax: 780–470–5687

Ermineskin Cree Nation
Box 249
Hobbema, AB T0C 1N0
Telephone: 780–585–2118
Fax: 780–585–2116

Frog Lake First Nation
General Delivery
Frog Lake, AB T0A 1M0
Telephone: 780–943–3912
Fax: 780–943–2336

Goodfish Lake First Nation
Box 275
Goodfish Lake, AB T0A 1R0
Telephone: 780–636–7011
Fax: 780–636–3534

Heart Lake First Nation
Box 1619
Lac La Biche, AB T0A 2C0
Telephone: 780–623–2330
Fax: 780–623–3505

Kehewin Cree Nation
Box 220
Kehewin, AB T0A 1C0
Telephone: 780–826–3333
Fax: 780–826–2355

Louis Bull First Nation
Box 1290
Hobbema, AB T0C 1N0
Telephone: 780–585–0036
Fax: 780–585–0039

Montana First Nation
Box 70
Hobbema, AB T0C 1N0
Telephone: 780–585–3744
Fax: 780–585–2264

O'Chiese First Nation
Box 1570
Rocky Mountain House, AB T4T 1B2
Telephone: 403–989–2034
Fax: 403–989–2122

Aboriginal Organizations and Agencies (continued)

Onion Lake First Nation
Box 340
Onion Lake, SK S0M 2E0
Telephone: 306–344–2525
Fax: 306–344–2559
Toll free: 1–888–344–8011

Paul First Nation Education
Box 84
Duffield, AB T0E 0N0
Telephone: 780–892–2025
Fax: 780–892–2019

Saddle Lake Cree Nation
Box 130
Saddle Lake, AB T0A 3T0
Telephone: 780–726–7641
Fax: 780–726–4069

Samson Cree Nation
Box 658
Hobbema, AB T0C 3T0
Telephone: 780–585–2211
Fax: 780–555–3857

Sunchild First Nation
Box 1149
Rocky Mountain House, AB
T0C 1N0
Telephone: 403–989–3476
Fax: 403–989–3614

Métis Settlements

Métis Settlements General Council
Suite 200, 10335 – 172 Street
Edmonton, AB T5S 1K9
Telephone: 780–822–4096
Fax: 780–489–9558
Toll free: 1–888–213–4400
Web site:
www.msgc.ca/MetisSettlement.htm

Métis Nation of Alberta
#100 Delia Gray Building
11738 Kingsway Avenue
Edmonton, AB T5G 0X5
Telephone: 780–455–2200
Fax: 780–452–8948
Toll free: 1–800–252–7553
Web site: www.metis.org

Additional Resources

Aboriginal Services Branch
Alberta Education
9th Floor, 44 Capital Boulevard
10044 – 108 Street
Edmonton, AB T5J 5E6
Telephone: 780–415–9300
Fax: 780–415–9306

For more information, see *A Guide to Aboriginal Organizations in Alberta* published by Aboriginal Affairs and Northern Development, available online at www.aand.gov.ab.ca/AAND.asp?lid=41.

Fishbone

Name _____

Date _____

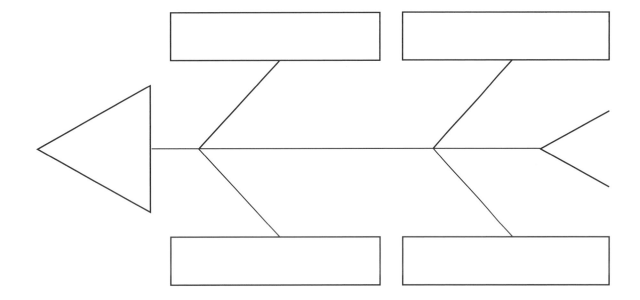

T-chart

Name _____

Date _____

Title/Topic: _____

Looks like:	Sounds like:	Feels like:

Venn Diagram

_____

Name _____

Date _____

_____

1. _____   _____

2. _____   _____

3. _____   _____

4. _____   _____

5. _____   _____

6. _____   _____

7. _____   _____

8. _____   _____

9. _____   _____

Differences   Similarities   Differences

P–M–I Chart

Name _____

Date _____

Topic: _____

Plus	Minus	Interesting Information

What do I think? Why?

Now that I have considered all the information, my thoughts on this topic are:

Place Mat

Name _____

Date _____

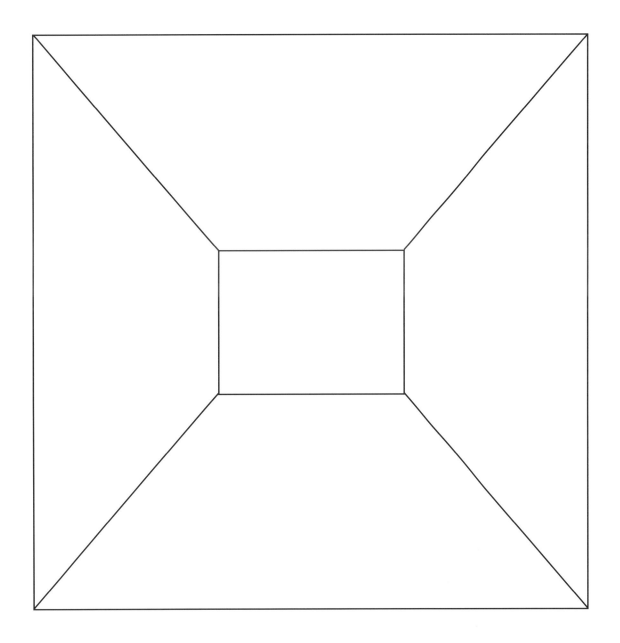

K–W–L Chart

Name _____

Date _____

K	W	L
(List what you already **know** about the topic.)	(List questions about what you **want to know** about the topic.)	(Using your questions as a guide, write all the information you **learned**.)

Brainstorm

Name _____

Date _____

Topic:

Goal _____   Time limit _____ minutes

Why am I doing this?

❑ to generate ideas   ❑ to make decisions
❑ to assess prior knowledge   ❑ to review information

1. _____
2. _____
3. _____
4. _____
5. _____
6. _____
7. _____
8. _____
9. _____
10. _____

Reflect and revise

❑ Are any ideas similar? If yes, combine similar ideas.
❑ Do all ideas fit the topic? If no, cross out ideas that don't fit.
❑ Star your three ideas.

Three-step Interview

Name _____

Date _____

Interview One: _____ (name)

_____

_____

_____

_____

Interview Two: _____ (name)

_____

_____

_____

_____

Interview Three: _____ (name)

_____

_____

_____

_____

Round Robin: Key ideas from interviews

_____

_____

_____

_____

_____

_____

Independent Study Planner

Name _____

Date _____

Why is this an important question?

(Rationale)

How can I show my learning?

(Product/format)

What is my critical question?

_____
_____
_____
_____
_____

Where can I look for information and answers?

(Sources)

When will I do **what**?

(Timeline)

Who ...

... has information?

... will review and discuss my project?

... will be my final audience?

Reproduced with permission from Edmonton Public Schools, *Think Again: Thinking Tools for Grades 6 to 10* (Edmonton, AB: Edmonton Public Schools, 2003), p. 182.

Choosing a Service Learning Project

Name _____

Date _____

Identified Need: _____

1. List reasons this is an important need for the class to address.

_____

_____

_____

2. What is one short-term project the class could do to address this need?

_____

_____

_____

3. What is needed for this project? (Think about expenses, materials, adult help, transportations.)

_____

_____

_____

4. What challenges or barriers might keep this project from being successful?

_____

_____

_____

5. What are *two* long-term projects the class might carry out to address this need?

_____

_____

_____

Adapted with permission from Lions Clubs International, *Skills for Adolescence: Service Learning* (4th edition) (Oak Brook, IL: Lions Clubs International Foundation, 2003), pp. 48–49.

Making It Happen

Service Learning Project Plan

Name _____

Date _____

1. The need we will address: _____
   _____

2. A brief description of our project: _____
   _____
   _____
   _____

3. Our project goals: _____
   _____
   _____
   _____

4. Our committee: _____
   _____
   _____
   _____

Jobs to be done	Who will do them?	Timelines
_____	_____	_____
_____	_____	_____
_____	_____	_____
_____	_____	_____
_____	_____	_____
_____	_____	_____
_____	_____	_____

Adapted with permission from Lions Clubs International, *Skills for Adolescence: Service Learning* (4th edition) (Oak Brook, IL: Lions Clubs International Foundation, 2003), p. 51.

Reflecting on Our Service Learning

Name _____

Date _____

1. What skills did the class use to carry out this project?

   _____
   _____
   _____
   _____
   _____
   _____

2. What was accomplished through this project?

   _____
   _____
   _____
   _____
   _____
   _____

3. What can we do to improve our next project?

   _____
   _____
   _____
   _____
   _____
   _____

Adapted with permission from Lions Clubs International, *Skills for Adolescence: Service Learning* (4th edition) (Oak Brook, IL: Lions Clubs International Foundation, 2003), p. 52.

Rubric Template

Student Name _____

Task _____

Date _____

Standard of excellence/outstanding evidence

-
-
-
-
-

Well on the way/strong evidence

-
-
-
-
-

Good start/some evidence

-
-
-
-
-

Just beginning/little evidence

-
-
-
-
-

Parents' Rights and Opportunities to Participate in Educational Decision Making

As a parent, you have rights and opportunities to participate in decision making about your child's education. You can do this by participating in the Individualized Program Planning (IPP) process for your child.

You have a right to:

- be involved in the decisions affecting your child's education

- learn about the school's programming and policies

- be consulted before your child is placed in a special education program

- learn about assessments that might help your child so you can give or deny your permission, in writing, for any formal assessment of your child

- be an informed and valued member of your child's Learning Circle. Circle members include parents, the student and teacher. It may also include other school staff, resource people and community members

- receive information on your child's learning and progress

- look at all the information in your child's school files

- appeal school decisions that you do not believe best serve the needs of your child. Talk to your school principal about your school district's or authority's appeal process. If you cannot resolve this disagreement at the local level, you have the right to request a Review by the Minister.

Adapted from Alberta Learning, *A Handbook for Aboriginal Parents of Children with Special Needs* (Edmonton, AB: Alberta Learning, 2000), pp. 3–4.

Transition Checklist

Name _____

Date _____

Use this transition checklist as you are moving from senior high to post-secondary studies.

I have:

- ❑ an updated copy of my last educational assessment
- ❑ a copy of my most recent Individualized Program Plan (IPP)
- ❑ copies of my high school transcripts
- ❑ any medical information I need to share
- ❑ a record of the assistive technology I have been using
- ❑ addresses and telephone numbers of the people who have provided assessment of my specific needs
- ❑ a summary of career searches/exploration I've completed
- ❑ contacted the special needs offices of the post-secondary institutions I am considering
- ❑ a copy of the accommodation policies of the post-secondary institutions I'm considering
- ❑ prepared a set of questions to ask about accommodations for my learning needs at these institutions
- ❑ prepared an inventory or portfolio of my successes and accomplishments at school and in the community
- ❑ visited the campuses (electronically or in person) of the institutions I'm considering
- ❑ information on funding sources and financial assistance opportunities
- ❑ completed the goals of my IPP transition plan.

Other information I will need:

- ❑ _____
- ❑ _____
- ❑ _____

Adapted from Calgary Learning Centre (Calgary, AB). Adapted with permission.

Decision-making Tree

Name _____

Date _____

Question

[ ]

Choice one

[ ]

Choice two

[ ]

What might happen

[ ]

What might happen

[ ]

My decision

[ ]

From Alberta Education, *Social Studies, Grades 1–3: Teacher Resource Manual* (Edmonton, AB: Alberta Education, 1989), p. 12.

Influences on Decision Making

Name _____

Date _____

Family   Peers

Decision to be made

_____

_____

_____

Values   Cultural beliefs

Questions you need to ask to help you make this decision

_____   _____

_____   _____

_____   _____

_____   _____

Adapted from Alberta Learning, *Kindergarten to Grade 9 Health and Life Skills Guide to Implementation* (Edmonton, AB: Alberta Learning, 2002), p. C.39.

Bibliography

Aboriginal Affairs and Northern Development. "Terms and Definitions. June 1, 2001. http://www.aand.gov.ab.ca/aand (Accessed July 2001).

Alberta Education. *Social Studies, Grades 1–3: Teacher Resource Manual.* Edmonton, AB: Alberta Education, 1989.

Alberta Education. *Teaching Students with Learning Disabilities.* Book 6 of the *Programming for Students with Special Needs* series. Edmonton, AB: Alberta Education, 1996.

Alberta Learning. *A Handbook for Aboriginal Parents of Children with Special Needs.* Edmonton, AB: Alberta Learning, 2000.

Alberta Learning. *Our Treasured Children* (video). Edmonton, AB: Alberta Learning, 2000.

Alberta Learning. *Make School Work for You: A Resource for Junior and Senior High Students Who Want to be More Successful Learners.* Edmonton, AB: Alberta Learning, 2001.

Alberta Learning. "Differentiating Instruction for Students with Learning Disabilities." In Alberta Learning, *Career and Life Management Guide to Implementation* (Edmonton, AB: Alberta Learning, 2002), pp. 91–108.

Alberta Learning. *Kindergarten to Grade 9 Health and Life Skills Guide to Implementation.* Edmonton, AB: Alberta Learning, 2002.

Alberta Learning. *First Nations, Métis and Inuit Education Policy Framework: A Progress Report.* Edmonton, AB: Alberta Learning, 2003.

Alberta Learning. *The Learning Team: A Handbook for Parents of Children with Special Needs.* Edmonton, AB: Alberta Learning, 2003.

Alberta Learning. *Unlocking Potential: Key Components of Programming for Students with Learning Disabilities.* Edmonton, AB: Alberta Learning, 2003.

Alberta Learning. *Standards for Special Education, Amended June 2004.* Edmonton, AB: Alberta Learning, 2004.

Alberta Learning. *Focus on Inquiry*. Edmonton, AB: Alberta Learning, 2004.

Alberta Teachers' Association. *Safe and Caring Schools for Aboriginal Students: A Guide for Teachers*. Edmonton, AB: The Alberta Teachers' Association, 2004.

Battiste, Marie. *Indigenous Knowledge and Pedagogy in First Nations Education: A Literature Review with Recommendations*. Ottawa, ON: Indian and Northern Affairs Canada, 2002.

Bennett, Barrie and Carol Rolheiser. *Beyond Monet: The Artful Science of Instructional Integration*. Toronto, ON: Bookation Inc., 2001.

Blackstock, Cindy with Marlyn Bennett. *National Children's Alliance Policy Paper on Aboriginal Children*. Ottawa, ON: National Children's Alliance, 2003.

Brendtro, Larry K., Martin Brokenleg and Steve Van Bockern. *Reclaiming Youth At Risk: Our Hope for the Future*. Bloomington, IN: National Educational Service, 1990.

Brizinski, Peggy. *Knots in a String: An Introduction to Native Studies in Canada*. Saskatoon, SK: Division of Extension and Community Relations, University of Saskatchewan, 1989.

Bryant, Diane Pedrotty and Brian R. Bryant. "Using Assistive Technology Adaptations to Include Students with Learning Disabilities in Cooperative Learning Activities." *Journal of Learning Disabilities* 31, 1 (1998), pp. 41–54.

Cajete, Gregory. *Look to the Mountain: An Ecology of Indigenous Education*. Durango, CO: Kivaki Press Inc., 1994.

Campbell, Maria. *Halfbreed*. Toronto, ON: McClelland and Stewart, 1973.

Canady, Robert Lynn and Phyllis Riley Hotchkiss. "It's A Good Score! Just A Bad Grade." *Phi Delta Kappan* 71, 1 (1989), pp. 68–71.

Cardinal, Harold and Walter Hildebrandt. *Treaty Elders of Saskatchewan: Our Dream is That Our Peoples Will One Day be Clearly Recognized as Nations*. Calgary, AB: University of Calgary Press, 2000.

Chamberlain, Steven B. "Recognizing and Responding to Cultural Differences in the Education of Culturally and Linguistically Diverse Learners." *Intervention in School and Clinic* 40, 4 (2005), pp. 195–211.

Chapman, Carolyn. *If the Shoe Fits...: How to Develop Multiple Intelligences in the Classroom.* Arlington Heights, IL: IRI/Skylight Training and Publishing Inc., 1993.

Dion, Joseph F. *My Tribe the Crees.* Calgary, AB: Glenbow-Alberta Institute, 1979.

DuPraw, Marcelle E. and Marya Axner. "Working on Common Cross-cultural Communication Challenges." 1997. www.wwcd.org/action/ampu/crosscult.html (Accessed June 2004).

Edmonton Public Schools. *Thinking Tools for Kids: Practical Organizers.* Edmonton, AB: Edmonton Public Schools, 1999.

Edmonton Public Schools. *Think Again: Thinking Tools for Grades 6 to 10.* Edmonton, AB: Edmonton Public Schools, 2003.

Farrell-Racette, Sherry et al. *Aboriginal Cultures and Perspectives: Making a Difference in the Classroom.* Number Five in the *Diversity in the Classroom Series.* Saskatoon, SK: Saskatchewan Professional Development Unit, and the Saskatchewan Instructional Development and Research Unit, 1996.

Fournier, Suzanne and Ernie Crey. *Stolen From Our Embrace: The Abduction of First Nations Children and the Restoration of Aboriginal Communities.* Vancouver, BC: Douglas and McIntyre Publishing Group, 1997.

Garrett, Michael Tlanusta. "Reflection by the Riverside: The Traditional Education of Native American Children." *Journal of Humanistic Education and Development* 35, 1 (1996), pp. 12–28.

Garrett, Michael Tlanusta. "'Two People': An American Indian Narrative of Bicultural Identity." *Journal of American Indian Education* 36, 1 (1996), pp. 1–21.

Garrett, Michael Tlanusta et al. "Open Hands, Open Hearts: Working with Native Youth in the Schools." *Intervention in School and Clinic* 38, 4 (2003), pp. 225–235.

Gilliland, Hap. *Teaching the Native American.* 4th edition. Dubuque, IA: Kendall/Hunt Publishing Co., 1999.

Government of Alberta. *Strengthening Relationships: The Government of Alberta's Aboriginal Policy Framework.* Edmonton, AB: Government of Alberta, 2000.

Hill, Diane. "Holistic Learning: A Model of Education Based on Aboriginal Cultural Philosophy." Unpublished master's thesis. St. Francis Xavier University, Antigonish, Nova Scotia, 1999.

Indian and Northern Affairs Canada. "Terminology." July 2003. http://www.ainc-inac.gc.ca/pr/info/tln_e.html (Accessed July 2005).

Indian and Northern Affairs Canada, and Statistics Canada. *Registered Indian Population Projections for Canada and Regions 2000–2021*. Ottawa, ON: Indian and Northern Affairs Canada, and Statistics Canada, n.d.

Kainai Board of Education et al. *Aboriginal Perspectives: Aboriginal Studies 10*. Edmonton, AB: Duval House Publishing Inc., 2004.

Kainai Board of Education et al. *Peoples and Cultural Change: Aboriginal Studies 20*. Edmonton, AB: Duval House Publishing Inc., 2005.

Kavanagh, Barbara. *The Role of Parental and Community Involvement in the Success of First Nations Learners: A Review of the Literature*. Ottawa, ON: Indian and Northern Affairs Canada, n.d.

Lions Clubs International. *Skills for Adolescence: Changes and Challenges* (4th edition). Oak Brook, IL: Lions Clubs International Foundation, 2003.

Lions Clubs International. *Skills for Adolescence: Service Learning* (4th edition). Oak Brook, IL: Lions Clubs International Foundation, 2003.

Mills, Sheryl. *Extending the Learning Community: Involving Parents and Families in Schools*. Saskatchewan School Trustees' Association (SSTA) Research Centre Report 94–09. Regina, SK: Saskatchewan School Trustees' Association, 1994.

O'Connor, Ken. *The Mindful School: How to Grade for Learning*. Arlington Heights, IL: Skylight Professional Development, 1999.

Ogle, Donna. "K–W–L: A Teaching Model that Develops Active Reading of Expository Text." *The Reading Teacher* 39, 6 (1986), pp. 564–571.

Rolheiser, Carol and John Ross. "Student Self-Evaluation—What Do We Know?" *Orbit* 30, 4 (2000), pp. 33–36.

Royal Commission on Aboriginal Peoples. *People to People, Nation to Nation: Highlights from the Royal Commission on Aboriginal Peoples*. Ottawa, ON: Minister of Supply and Services Canada, 1996a.

Royal Commission on Aboriginal Peoples. *Report of the Royal Commission on Aboriginal Peoples – Volume 1: Looking Forward, Looking Back.* Ottawa, ON: Minister of Supply and Services Canada, 1996b.

Royal Commission on Aboriginal Peoples. *Report of the Royal Commission on Aboriginal Peoples – Volume 3: Gathering Strength.* Ottawa, ON: Minister of Supply and Services Canada, 1996c.

Scott, Duncan Campbell. "Indian Affairs, 1867–1912." In Adam Shortt and Arthur G. Doughty (eds.), *Canada and its Provinces: A History of the Canadian People and Their Institutions by One Hundred Associates* (Toronto, ON: Glasgow, Brook and Company, 1913), Volume VII, pp. 593–628.

Seita, John R. and Larry K. Brendtro. *Kids Who Outwit Adults.* Longmont, CO: Sopris West, 2002.

Swanson, Sharon. "Motivating Learners in Northern Communities." *Canadian Journal of Native Education* 27, 1 (2003), pp. 61–73.

Tafoya, Terry. "Finding Harmony: Balancing Traditional Values with Western Science in Therapy." *Canadian Journal of Native Education* 21, Supplement (1995), pp. 7–27.

Walker, Catherine and Edgar Schmidt. *Smart Tests: Teacher-made Tests that Help Students Learn.* Markham, ON: Pembroke Publishers, 2004.

Western Canadian Protocol for Collaboration in Basic Education. *The Common Curriculum Framework for Aboriginal Language and Culture Programs: Kindergarten to Grade 12.* Western Canadian Protocol for Collaboration in Basic Education, 2000.

Wilson, Stan. "The Great Divide: Whitestream Teachers and Aboriginal Students." Unpublished paper presented at Greater Edmonton Teachers' Convention, Edmonton, Alberta, February 2001.

Index

OUR WORDS, OUR WAYS

OUR WORDS, OUR WAYS

OUR WORDS, OUR WAYS
© Alberta Education, Alberta, Canada

Feedback

Our Words, Our Ways: Teaching First Nations, Métis and Inuit Learners (2005)

We hope this resource is helpful in enhancing the success of Aboriginal students in your school. Please indicate your agreement with the following statements about this resource.

Please return this page to:
Alberta Education
Learning and Teaching Resources
  Branch
8ᵗʰ Floor, 44 Capital Boulevard
10044 – 108 Street
Edmonton, AB T5J 5E6
Fax: 780–422–0576

1. This resource contains practical information that school staff can use for supporting and enhancing the success of Aboriginal students in their schools and classrooms.

   ○ strongly agree ○ agree   ○ disagree ○ strongly disagree

   COMMENTS

   _____

   _____

   _____

2. This resource is well-organized, and easy to read and use.

   ○ strongly agree ○ agree   ○ disagree ○ strongly disagree

   COMMENTS

   _____

   _____

   _____

3. The information in this resource enhanced my understanding of strategies that could enhance the success of Aboriginal students.

   ○ strongly agree ○ agree   ○ disagree ○ strongly disagree

   COMMENTS

   _____

   _____

   _____

4. We welcome your comments and suggestions for future Alberta Education resources.

   COMMENTS

   _____

   _____

   _____

215

Our Words, Our Ways: Teaching First Nations, Métis and Inuit Learners

This resource offers information and sample strategies that classroom teachers can use to help their Aboriginal students be successful learners. It provides information on Aboriginal cultures and perspectives, and discusses the importance of family and community involvement. It includes shared wisdom from Elders and Aboriginal scholars, and related stories shared by teachers of Aboriginal students. The resource also includes information on learning disabilities and recognizing the gifts of individual students.

 This resource is also available for downloading at no cost from:
http://www.education.gov.ab.ca/k_12/curriculum/other.asp

Order form → Please mail this order form to the **Learning Resources Centre** (LRC), 12360 – 142 Street, Edmonton, AB, T5L 4X9 or fax it to 780–422–9750

Please send _____ copy(ies) of *Our Words, Our Ways: Teaching First Nations, Métis and Inuit Learners* (2005)
Order #619166   **$10.20** + GST (**Please note:** Price subject to change)

                                         Total cost $_____

Ship to:

Name: _____

Address: _____

_____

City: _____   Province: _____   Postal Code: _____

Telephone: _____   Fax: _____

Method of payment:

☐ Cheque/money order enclosed   ☐ Purchase order enclosed P.O. # _____

☐ VISA/MasterCard # _____   Expiry date: _____

   Customer signature _____

---

* Eligible School Authorities can apply the 25% Learning Resources Credit Allocation (LRCA) toward the purchase of this resource (* some restrictions apply). Contact the LRC, Customer Service, for more information at 780–427–2767; fax 780–422–9750.

The LRC offers online ordering at http://www.lrc.education.gov.ab.ca/   © September 2005